COMPACT *Research*

Influenza

Diseases and Disorders

ReferencePoint
Press®

San Diego, CA

Select* books in the Compact Research series include:

Current Issues
Abortion
Animal Experimentation
Conflict in the Middle East
DNA Evidence and
   Investigation
Drugs and Sports
Gangs
Genetic Testing
Gun Control
Immigration

Islam
National Security
Nuclear Weapons and
   Security
Obesity
Stem Cells
Teen Smoking
Terrorist Attacks
Video Games

Diseases and Disorders
ADHD
Anorexia
Autism
Bipolar Disorders
Drug Addiction
HPV
Mood Disorders

Obsessive-Compulsive
   Disorder
Phobias
Post-Traumatic Stress
   Disorder
Self-Injury Disorder
Sexually Transmitted
   Diseases

Drugs
Antidepressants
Club Drugs
Cocaine and Crack
Hallucinogens
Heroin
Inhalants
Marijuana

Methamphetamine
Nicotine and Tobacco
Painkillers
Performance-Enhancing
   Drugs
Prescription Drugs
Steroids

Energy and the Environment
Biofuels
Coal Power
Deforestation
Energy Alternatives
Garbage and Recycling
Global Warming and
   Climate Change

Hydrogen Power
Nuclear Power
Solar Power
Toxic Waste
Wind Power
World Energy Crisis

*For a complete list of titles please visit www.referencepointpress.com.

COMPACT *Research*

Influenza

Peggy J. Parks

Diseases and Disorders

ReferencePoint
Press®

San Diego, CA

© 2011 ReferencePoint Press, Inc.

For more information, contact:
ReferencePoint Press, Inc.
PO Box 27779
San Diego, CA 92198
www.ReferencePointPress.com

Picture credits:
Cover: Dreamstime and iStockphoto.com
Maury Aaseng: 33–34, 45–47, 60–61, 74–76
AP Images: 19
Science Photo Library: 12

LIBRARY OF CONGRESS CATALOGING-IN-PUBLICATION DATA

Parks, Peggy J., 1951–
    Influenza / by Peggy J. Parks.
      p. cm. — (Compact research series)
    Includes bibliographical references and index.
    ISBN-13: 978-1-60152-118-7 (hardback)
    ISBN-10: 1-60152-118-9 (hardback)
    1. Influenza—Juvenile literature. 2. H1N1 influenza—Juvenile literature. I. Title.
    RC150.P37   2010
    616.2'03—-dc22

                                                                          2010026063

Contents

Foreword

❝Where is the knowledge we have lost in information?❞

—T.S. Eliot, "The Rock."

As modern civilization continues to evolve, its ability to create, store, distribute, and access information expands exponentially. The explosion of information from all media continues to increase at a phenomenal rate. By 2020 some experts predict the worldwide information base will double every 73 days. While access to diverse sources of information and perspectives is paramount to any democratic society, information alone cannot help people gain knowledge and understanding. Information must be organized and presented clearly and succinctly in order to be understood. The challenge in the digital age becomes not the creation of information, but how best to sort, organize, enhance, and present information.

ReferencePoint Press developed the *Compact Research* series with this challenge of the information age in mind. More than any other subject area today, researching current issues can yield vast, diverse, and unqualified information that can be intimidating and overwhelming for even the most advanced and motivated researcher. The *Compact Research* series offers a compact, relevant, intelligent, and conveniently organized collection of information covering a variety of current topics ranging from illegal immigration and deforestation to diseases such as anorexia and meningitis.

The series focuses on three types of information: objective single-author narratives, opinion-based primary source quotations, and facts and statistics. The clearly written objective narratives provide context and reliable background information. Primary source quotes are carefully selected and cited, exposing the reader to differing points of view. And facts and statistics sections aid the reader in evaluating perspectives. Presenting these key types of information creates a richer, more balanced learning experience.

For better understanding and convenience, the series enhances information by organizing it into narrower topics and adding design features that make it easy for a reader to identify desired content. For example, in *Compact Research: Illegal Immigration*, a chapter covering the economic impact of illegal immigration has an objective narrative explaining the various ways the economy is impacted, a balanced section of numerous primary source quotes on the topic, followed by facts and full-color illustrations to encourage evaluation of contrasting perspectives.

The ancient Roman philosopher Lucius Annaeus Seneca wrote, "It is quality rather than quantity that matters." More than just a collection of content, the *Compact Research* series is simply committed to creating, finding, organizing, and presenting the most relevant and appropriate amount of information on a current topic in a user-friendly style that invites, intrigues, and fosters understanding.

Influenza at a Glance

What Is Influenza?

Influenza is an acute viral infection of the respiratory system.

Flu Statistics

The Centers for Disease Control and Prevention estimates that 1 out of 5 Americans is infected with influenza each year, 226,000 are hospitalized, and 36,000 die from influenza and flu-related complications.

Symptoms

People with influenza often suffer from high fever, sore throat, dry cough, headache, body aches, and extreme fatigue.

Cause

Influenza is caused by viruses, which are categorized as type A, B, and C. Type A flu viruses are divided into subtypes and cause the most serious cases of influenza.

People at Risk

Those with the highest risk of seasonal influenza infection include people over the age of 65, pregnant women, people with chronic health problems, and young children. The 2009 H1N1 influenza virus has proved most threatening to school-age children and young adults.

How Influenza Spreads

Influenza is most commonly transmitted from person to person when those who are infected cough or sneeze and infectious droplets pass through the air. It also spreads when viral particles are deposited onto hard surfaces and touched by someone else.

Diagnosis and Treatment

Influenza can be diagnosed through laboratory tests. Treatments include plenty of bed rest and increased intake of fluids, as well as antiviral drugs.

Flu Season

Influenza season typically occurs during the winter months: from November to April in the Northern Hemisphere and from May through September in the Southern Hemisphere.

Pandemics

A pandemic is a widespread disease outbreak, often spreading to many parts of the world. Pandemic types of influenza are those created by viruses that are newly formed and not seen in humans before.

Preventing Outbreaks

Public health officials state that the best way to prevent influenza infection is to have an annual flu vaccination, with a second one during pandemic years. Other precautionary measures include frequent hand washing and use of hand sanitizers.

Overview

66 **Influenza has caused recurrent disease outbreaks for centuries, as has been well documented in our historical literature.** 99

—Roni K. Devlin, a physician who specializes in infectious diseases.

66 **The term *influenza* is derived from Italian and was first used in the Middle Ages when the illness was thought to be due to the unfavorable 'influences' of our stars! You won't find that today in the astrology pages of a newspaper.** 99

—Terence Stephenson, president of the Royal College of Paediatrics and Child Health in the United Kingdom.

Kelsey Young was thrilled to learn that she was pregnant with her first child. The 20-year-old expectant mother was so excited that she planned her own baby shower and filled a closet with baby clothes. During the thirty-second week of her pregnancy, Young began feeling ill and feverish and was having trouble breathing. She was admitted to a hospital, where doctors diagnosed pneumonia and recommended that she have a cesarean section in order to help her body recover.

On August 27, 2009, Young gave birth to a baby girl whom she named Ava Renee. After the baby was born, and while Young was still hospitalized, tests showed that she was suffering from a severe respiratory illness known as H1N1 influenza (formerly called swine flu). At first she seemed to be recovering, but then her health quickly began to deteriorate. One week later Young was dead. "It's really sad that she's gone," says her sister Mandy Quinn, "and I think the biggest thing that's really hitting our family now at this point is that baby Ava is never going to be able to meet her mother." Quinn says that people need to understand how serious H1N1 influenza can be, adding, "You know, people may think the media has kind of overblown this and you know that's what we thought for a while, that it was just overblown, but then it hit our family and it's a real thing, it's a real threat and we don't want anybody else to have to go through this."[1]

What Is Influenza?

The word *influenza* has two meanings: It refers to an acute infection of the respiratory system as well as to the viruses that cause the infection. The disease known as influenza (commonly called "the flu") affects people in different ways, with physical symptoms ranging from relatively mild to severe enough to be life-threatening. Unlike colds, which tend to develop gradually, influenza can strike without warning, with a sudden onset of fever, sore throat, dry cough, headache, and body aches. As the National Institute of Allergy and Infectious Diseases explains: "The flu differs in several ways from the common cold. For example, people with colds rarely get fevers or headaches or suffer from the extreme exhaustion that flu viruses cause. The most familiar aspect of the flu is the way it can 'knock you off your feet' as it sweeps through entire communities."[2]

> **Thousands of viruses exist, and they are among the smallest infectious objects known to scientists—so tiny that they cannot be seen with an ordinary microscope.**

The terms "stomach flu" or "24-hour flu bug" are commonly used when people suffer from a short bout of achiness, vomiting, stomach cramps, and diarrhea. Yet as sick and miserable as they may feel, this sort of illness is not the same as influenza. As the Centers for Disease Control and Prevention (CDC) explains: "These symptoms can be caused by many different viruses, bacteria or even parasites. While vomiting, diarrhea, and being nauseous or 'sick to your stomach' can sometimes be related to the

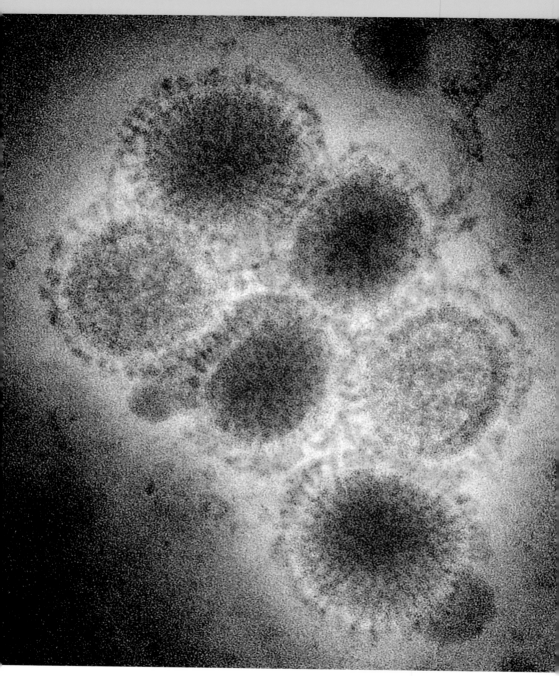

The H1N1 virus, seen here in a colored electron micrograph, was responsible for the influenza pandemic that originated in Mexico in 2009. Although H1N1 killed thousands of people worldwide, seasonal flu kills many more people every year.

flu—more commonly in children than adults—these problems are rarely the main symptoms of influenza. The flu is a respiratory disease and not a stomach or intestinal disease."[3]

What Causes Influenza?

Numerous diseases are caused by bacteria, and for many years scientists were convinced that the same was true of influenza. This was an erroneous belief, however, as influenza specialist Charles Davis explains: "*Haemophilus influenzae* is a bacterium that was incorrectly considered to cause the flu until the virus was demonstrated to be the correct cause. . . . This bacterium can cause lung infections in infants and children, and it occasionally causes ear, eye, sinus, joint, and a few other infections, but it does not cause the flu."[4] Davis's reference to the "correct cause" refers to discoveries made in the 1930s by American and British scientists. After performing a number of experiments, they confirmed that viruses rather than bacteria are responsible for influenza. Later studies showed that viruses also cause avian influenza, which affects poultry and wild birds.

In order to understand how viruses cause influenza, it is important to know more about viruses. Thousands of viruses exist, and they are among the smallest infectious objects known to scientists—so tiny that they cannot be seen with an ordinary microscope. Instead, viruses can only be examined with electron microscopes, which are highly sensitive instruments that use electrons to magnify objects up to about 1,000 times larger than is possible with a light microscope. Medical journalist Delthia Ricks, the author of *100 Questions & Answers About Influenza*, describes these minuscule entities: "Magnified with the aid of an electron microscope, a flu virus looks like a mere fluff of protein stippled with a multitude of tiny spikes. Imagine a miniature mace, the medieval weapon, a metal ball with dozens of spikes—that's basically a flu virus up close and personal."[5]

Viruses have the ability to infect everything from plants to animals,

> " Of the three main influenza types, viruses in the A category are the most common—and by far the most dangerous. "

and even bacteria. According to British pediatrician Terence Stephenson, viruses exist everywhere on earth and are "the most abundant living thing on the planet."[6] One unique characteristic of viruses is that they exist for one purpose only: to make more viruses. But since they have no ability to reproduce on their own, they must invade the cells of a living organism known as a host. The viruses use the host cells' reproductive mechanism to manufacture new viral particles, which then burst out of the cells and travel along the bloodstream in search of other cells to infect.

Like all viruses, those associated with influenza are highly selective about which cells they choose to invade. In humans and other mammals, the viruses prefer to attack the respiratory system. In wild birds and poultry, they target the gastrointestinal system.

Influenza ABCs

Scientists have learned that more than one virus causes influenza, with the three major types being A, B, and C. Type A influenza viruses have been further divided into subtypes based on differences in two proteins that are present on a virus's surface: hemagglutinin (H or HA), which enables a virus to stick to a cell and initiate infection, and neuraminidase (N or NA), whose function is to help newly formed viral particles break free from host cells. Over years of research, a total of 16 known H influenza subtypes (H1 to H16) and 9 N subtypes (N1 to N9) have been identified.

The code name that is given to each influenza virus reflects the variations of its proteins. For example, an H1N1 influenza virus indicates the presence of an H1 protein and an N1 protein, while an H3N2 virus has an H3 protein and an N2 protein. Ricks explains the purpose of this coding: "Labeling Type A subtypes with *H* and *N* along with very specific numbers is yet another way scientists further identify Type

> **Anywhere people congregate— schools, office buildings, auditoriums, subways, shopping malls, airports, or any other enclosed space—can become a breeding ground for virus transmission and influenza infection.**

A viruses."[7] According to the CDC, as of June 2010, 3 influenza A subtypes were circulating among humans: H1N1, H1N2, and H3N2.

Of the three main influenza types, viruses in the A category are the most common—and by far the most dangerous. Type A influenza viruses are directly responsible for the deadliest outbreaks in history. "Historically," writes Ricks, "it has been Type A viruses that have triggered globe-sweeping pandemics. Indeed, all of the strains that caused worldwide pandemics and unusually high mortality in the 20th century were Type A influenza viruses."[8]

> " Health experts have observed that [H1N1] influenza has been far more prevalent among otherwise healthy children and young adults than is normally observed with seasonal flu strains. "

Viruses in the B category cause outbreaks every three to five years. Although this type of flu can make people feel very sick, type B viruses do not typically result in illness that is as severe as type A. Type B influenza does, however, cause widespread epidemics, as infectious disease physician Roni K. Devlin explains: "Often, the outbreaks of influenza B are reported in schools, military camps, chronic-care facilities, and nursing homes; it has also caused at least one identified outbreak on a cruise ship."[9] Even though type B influenza epidemics are relatively common, the viruses have not been linked to pandemics. Nor have type C viruses, which are considered the tamest of all influenza types. Type C viruses often cause illness that is similar to a common cold, and they typically result in milder outbreaks that do not become epidemics.

The Spread of Influenza

Influenza is an extremely contagious disease. The virus is transmitted from person to person (known as viral shedding) when someone who is infected coughs, sneezes, or even talks or laughs around others. In a phenomenon called droplet spread, virus-laden microscopic drops—up to 40,000 of which can be released in a single sneeze—are propelled through the air and breathed in by anyone who is nearby. This happens most frequently when someone with influenza is sick and exhibiting symptoms, but infection can also occur prior to that. Influenza is contagious about a day or two before symptoms appear, which is known as the incubation period. According to Devlin, children with influenza are contagious even longer than adults. She writes: "They may begin shedding the virus days before symptoms occur and continue to shed for more than ten days beyond the active phase of illness."[10]

Because influenza is so contagious, infection can occur on a massive scale. Anywhere people congregate—schools, office buildings, auditoriums, subways, shopping malls, airports, or any other enclosed space—can become a breeding ground for virus transmission and influenza infection. Studies have shown that one person with influenza can infect at least two others, and that influenza spreads fast in closed areas. International travel is a huge factor in the spread of influenza, as Ricks explains: "With airlines worldwide moving millions of people daily from one part of the globe to another, it should come as no surprise that contagious illnesses occurring in one part of the world can be easily transported to another in a matter of a few hours."[11]

> " One type of influenza test that has been in use since 2007 can produce a diagnosis in as little as 30 minutes, compared with older tests that took up to 5 days. "

In addition to direct person-to-person contact, influenza also spreads when viral particles are deposited onto objects such as computer keyboards, tabletops, doorknobs, TV remotes, or telephones. Those who touch the contaminated objects may become infected when they rub their eyes or touch their noses or mouths. Influenza viruses can survive on surfaces for anywhere from a few minutes to more than eight hours, although the amount of time can vary depending on the type of surface. Mayo Clinic physician James M. Steckelberg explains:

> Researchers have repeatedly found that cold and flu germs generally remain active longer on stainless steel, plastic and similar hard surfaces than on fabric and other

soft surfaces. On any surface, though, flu viruses seem to live longer than cold viruses do. Other factors, such as the amount of virus deposited on a surface and the temperature and humidity of the environment, also have effects on how long cold and flu germs stay active outside the body.[12]

Influenza's Victims

Males and females of all ages, races, cultures, and walks of life may be stricken with influenza, but certain people are at higher risk of being infected and becoming seriously ill. This includes adults over the age of 65; people with weakened immune systems; those who suffer from chronic medical conditions such as asthma, diabetes, or heart disease; pregnant women; and children, especially those who are under six years old.

With seasonal influenza epidemics, elderly people are considered to have the highest risk of becoming sick and developing severe complications, as well as the highest death rate. But this has not proved to be true with the H1N1 strain that emerged in 2009. Health experts have observed that this type of influenza has been far more prevalent among otherwise healthy children and young adults than is normally observed with seasonal flu strains. As U.S. assistant surgeon general Anne Schuchat explains: "I think it's very important to put in contrast what we've seen so far this year with the 2009 H1N1 pandemic virus and what we typically will see in a seasonal influenza. . . . There's a shift to younger people in terms of serious illness, hospitalization, and death. And that does make it different."[13]

Diagnosis and Treatment of Influenza

The first step in arriving at a flu diagnosis is a physical examination, but it is often difficult for physicians to distinguish influenza from other types of infections solely based on symptoms. One reason for this is that many respiratory diseases can mimic the symptoms of influenza, making it challenging to tell one from another. That is where diagnostic testing is valuable, as Devlin explains: "Using laboratory tests to confirm the diagnosis of influenza if it is suspected by the findings of the health history and physical examination can lead to more appropriate treatment recommendations. The laboratory diagnosis of influenza is also important to helping to prevent, contain, monitor, and treat the illness."[14]

One type of influenza test that has been in use since 2007 can produce a diagnosis in as little as 30 minutes, compared with older tests that took up to 5 days. It involves taking a swab from a patient, often from the back of the nose, and combining the specimen with chemicals. Drops of the solution are applied to a test strip, and if a certain color (such as pinkish purple) appears, this indicates a positive result for influenza.

Treatment for influenza varies based on the patient and the severity of his or her illness. As with any other viral infection, physicians often recommend that people suffering from the flu get plenty of bed rest, drink fluids, and take over-the-counter pain relievers as needed for fever and body aches. If influenza is diagnosed within the first few days of the appearance of symptoms, antiviral medications such as Tamiflu may be prescribed. These drugs work by deactivating an enzyme that viruses need to reproduce, thus inhibiting their ability to grow and spread. And while antivirals do not cure influenza, they can reduce the severity of flu symptoms and shorten the time someone is sick by one or two days.

What Are the Public Health Risks of Influenza?

Most people who become sick with influenza feel better within a week or two. But for others, the flu can be a life-threatening illness. Devlin explains:

> In some lucky patients, little to no symptoms are ever appreciated, even beyond the incubation period. In most others, however, an abrupt onset of symptoms occurs once the incubation period is complete, signifying full activation of the immune defense system. Some cases of influenza remain uncomplicated, whereas others progress to more worrisome and severe manifestations or even death.[15]

The most common health risk posed by influenza is pneumonia, which is a serious infection of the lungs. Severe cases of the flu can progress into viral pneumonia, while bacterial pneumonia occurs when someone's immune system has been so badly weakened that bacteria invade the lungs and the body cannot fight off the resulting infection. Influenza can also make chronic medical conditions worse. For instance, people with influenza who suffer from asthma may experience asthma attacks

Hundreds wait for H1N1 vaccines at a clinic in Maryland in October 2009. Public health officials urged Americans to get vaccinated but with limited supplies the vaccines went first to those most at risk, including children, teenagers, and pregnant women.

while they are sick. In those with chronic congestive heart failure, the flu may trigger symptoms that worsen their condition.

Imprecise Statistics

The CDC says that on average, 36,000 people in the United States die each year from influenza and related causes. Yet that number is only an estimate, because there is no way to determine the exact number of deaths with any certainty. There are several reasons for this, as the CDC explains:

> Some deaths—particularly in the elderly—are associated with secondary complications of seasonal influenza (including bacterial pneumonias). Influenza virus infection

may not be identified in many instances because influenza virus is only detectable for a short period of time and many people don't seek medical care until after the first few days of acute illness. For these reasons, statistical modeling strategies have been used to estimate seasonal flu–related deaths for many decades, both in the United States and the United Kingdom.[16]

The CDC adds that only counting deaths where influenza was listed on a death certificate would greatly underestimate the true impact of seasonal influenza.

A prime example of extreme variations in flu-related statistics is the CDC's estimate of people who died from the new H1N1 influenza strain between April 2009 and April 2010. The number of U.S. deaths from H1N1 ranges from a low of 8,870 to a high of 18,300. Statistics from the World Health Organization are also not precise, because the group relies on its member nations to provide information about influenza illness and deaths. In its report dated June 11, 2010, WHO states that laboratory-confirmed deaths worldwide from 2009 H1N1 exceed 18,156. That is undoubtedly far below the actual total, as it is lower than the maximum estimate of deaths in the United States alone.

> " A prime example of extreme variations in flu-related statistics is the CDC's estimate of people who died from the new H1N1 influenza strain between April 2009 and April 2010. "

How Can Influenza Outbreaks Be Prevented?

Even though medical science has vastly improved survival rates, influenza remains a disease that is neither curable nor 100 percent preventable. One of the biggest challenges is how contagious it is and how easily and rapidly it can be passed from one person to another. People can, however, substantially reduce their risk of being infected by taking precautions such as washing their hands frequently with soap and water, avoiding large crowds during flu season, and keeping away from individuals who are known to be infected.

Another important precautionary measure is getting the recommended flu vaccination each year. The World Health Organization states that among healthy adults, the influenza vaccine can prevent from 70 to 90 percent of influenza cases. Among the elderly, vaccination can reduce the number of influenza-related deaths by as much as 80 percent. When a pandemic flu vaccine is available, such as the one developed in 2009 for H1N1 influenza, a second vaccination is recommended for optimum protection.

Ongoing Challenges

Over the years, research has yielded a great deal of scientific knowledge about influenza, including the development of vaccinations that help prevent it and drugs that help relieve symptoms. Challenges remain, however, as the flu is still a deadly disease that sickens and kills people all over the world year after year. As scientists continue to study it, their research may someday yield discoveries that make influenza a thing of the past.

What Is Influenza?

66Even an average case of flu can knock you on your back. It's no picnic. You can lose a few days of work or school, and, in serious or severe cases, [it] can send you to the hospital, or, tragically, can result in death.99

—Thomas Frieden, director of the Centers for Disease Control and Prevention.

66Flu should never be dismissed as 'just the flu.' It's a serious disease, and while most cases are mild, some can be deadly.99

—U.S. Department of Health and Human Services.

Influenza sickens millions of people each year, and according to the World Health Organization, claims as many as 500,000 lives worldwide. Yet in spite of such grim statistics, the disease is widely misunderstood and often not taken seriously. Many people are either unaware of how deadly influenza can be or do not think they are at risk of being infected with it. Delthia Ricks writes:

> Even with a reputation for circling the globe, many people consider influenza to be nothing more than a wintertime annoyance, something that arrives with other unavoidable seasonal nuisances: cold weather, bulkier clothing, and higher home heating bills. Television commercials also seem to have downgraded the importance of influenza by giving it second billing in so-called cold and flu season.[17]

Public Apathy

Surveys have consistently shown that many Americans have a lackadaisical attitude about influenza, including H1N1 flu. This became apparent during a comprehensive review of 20 national polls that were conducted between April 2009 and January 2010. The purposes of the review were to determine whether people had adopted specific behaviors during certain periods of the pandemic and to examine the reasons why many chose not to get vaccinated. The researchers who performed the study found that a substantial number of respondents had no intention of getting the H1N1 vaccination, with a major reason being their belief that such a precaution was not needed. Close to 50 percent of respondents said they were not worried about getting a serious case of H1N1 influenza.

In addition, 27 percent of parents surveyed said they would not, or might not, have their children vaccinated. When asked their reason for that decision, they said they did not believe the children were at risk for developing H1N1. The study's authors write: "Our review of these data suggests that in the event of a future influenza pandemic, a substantial proportion of the public may not take a newly developed vaccine. . . . More work may need to be done to understand the basis of these beliefs and to address them in the case of a serious influenza outbreak."[18]

> " Surveys have consistently shown that many Americans have a lackadaisical attitude about influenza, including H1N1 flu. "

Viruses on Attack

In humans and other mammals, influenza viruses prefer to attack the respiratory system. This viral invasion kills the tiny cells in the lining of the airways and leads to inflammation, causing the lining to thicken and become red and sore. Terence Stephenson describes the effect: "The lining of the airways consists of 'hair cells,' tiny cilia which beat back and forward, sweeping dust, bugs and other debris up from the lungs and airways as mucus, keeping them clean. If this 'muco-ciliary escalator' is damaged, mucus and secretions collect in our airways and we sniffle, cough and sneeze in an effort to eject the fluid."[19]

The inflammation first spreads into the mucous membrane that lines the nose, causing a condition known as rhinitis. Then it continues its journey down the throat and windpipe. In the most severe cases, the inflammation moves all the way down in the lungs, beyond the small airways and deep into lung tissue, which results in viral pneumonia. Stephenson writes: "Pneumonia literally means lung infection, commonly called a chest infection. This can interfere with the ability of the lungs to get oxygen into the body and provides the perfect environment for bacteria to creep in as unwanted guests."[20]

According to a study published in September 2009, serious infections are more likely in people who are suffering from H1N1 influenza than from seasonal flu strains. Researchers from the United Kingdom examined the way the two types of flu viruses attached to receptors, which are beadlike molecules on the outside of cells. All influenza viruses bind to receptors, but those of the seasonal type only attach to cells in the nose, throat, and upper airway. The team found that the H1N1 viruses also attached to receptors located deep inside the lungs, which could explain why many people infected with H1N1 suffer from more severe symptoms than those with seasonal influenza. As researcher Ted Feizi explains:

> Most people infected with swine-origin flu in the current pandemic have experienced relatively mild symptoms. However, some people have had more severe lung infections, which can be worse than those caused by seasonal flu. Our new research shows how the virus does this—by attaching to receptors mostly found on cells deep in the lungs. This is something seasonal flu cannot do.[21]

A Winter Disease

Each year, with highly predictable regularity, flu season arrives and influenza sickens millions of people worldwide. The World Health Organization states that these annual epidemics result in about 3 to 5 million cases of severe illness per year. According to the CDC, an estimated 5 to 20 percent of Americans are infected during seasonal influenza outbreaks, with more than 200,000 people becoming sick enough to require hospitalization. Influenza season typically occurs during the winter months, which last from November to April in the Northern Hemisphere (with the heaviest influenza activity during the month of February), and from May through September in the Southern Hemisphere.

The fact that seasonal influenza spreads most voraciously during the cold winter months has been mysterious to scientists for years. On its most basic level, this seems to make sense: Winter is when people tend to stay indoors and cluster together, which provides greater opportunities for viruses to be passed around. A primary example is schools,

> " According to a study published in September 2009, serious infections are more likely in people who are suffering from H1N1 influenza than from seasonal flu strains. "

as influenza researcher Jonathan McCullers explains: "We know one of the largest factors is kids in school—most of the major epidemics are traced to children."[22]

Yet like a number of other researchers, McCullers rejects the "more time spent indoors" theory as an explanation for why influenza outbreaks are more intense during the winter months, as he states: "That never made sense."[23] McCullers reasons that school is in session in September and October, and influenza is rarely seen during those months. Also, people work throughout the entire year, including spring, summer, and fall. They crowd into buses, subways, and planes, go to the theater, eat in restaurants, and gather in innumerable other venues, no matter what the season is. So why winter?

A study published in October 2007 by researchers from New York's Mount Sinai School of Medicine may have provided the answer to that question. In an experiment, researchers exposed guinea pigs to the influenza virus in a temperature-controlled environment. By varying the air temperature, the team found that the virus spread much more rapidly at a relatively cool 41°F (5°C). As the temperature slowly increased, infections began to decline, with viral transmission stopping altogether at 86°F (30°C). In addition, the virus spread best when the humidity was low, at about 20 percent, and did not spread in 80 percent humidity.

From this study the team concluded that influenza viruses are more stable in cold, dry weather. Low humidity likely pulls moisture out of virus-laden droplets in the air, helping them to remain suspended. As influenza researcher Peter Palese explains: "The virus is probably more stable in cold temperature, so it hangs in the air much longer."[24]

> The fact that seasonal influenza spreads most voraciously during the cold winter months has been mysterious to scientists for years.

Although seasonal influenza strikes like clockwork during the winter months, the same is not true of flu strains that lead to pandemics. They are unpredictable, striking any time of the year rather than only during winter. Although this has long been puzzling to scientists, Jeffery K. Taubenberger, a virologist and a world-renowned influenza expert, has a theory about it. Based on research about major flu pandemics from the past, Taubenberger suggests that pandemic flu strains may smolder for months or even years before an outbreak occurs. If he is correct, this could possibly explain why the 2009 H1N1 influenza emerged in April rather than during winter months. Perhaps the virus had been smoldering for a long time before people were infected.

A Close Brush with Death

One characteristic of H1N1 influenza that is worrisome to public health officials is how the flu strain has targeted children, teenagers, and adults under the age of 30, while largely sparing older people. According to the CDC, more than three-fourths of the cases have affected those under the age of 30, with the highest number among children and teenagers aged 10 to 19. Michael Osterholm, the director of the University of Minnesota's Center for Infectious Disease Research and Policy, explains: "This virus does do damage differently than seasonal flu. We're talking about a disease that causes severe disease and deaths in a much younger population where you don't expect to see that."[25]

One teenager who was stricken with H1N1 influenza was Luke Duvall, a 15-year-old high school sophomore from Atkins, Arkansas—and the disease came perilously close to killing him. An all-star athlete who was in top physical condition, Duvall was playing in a football game on the evening of October 2, 2009. Although the game had just begun, he was already exhausted and so cold that he could not wait to get in the car and blast the heater. After the game was over, Duvall went home and crawled into bed, assuming that he was just having a bad night. The next morning there was no doubt how wrong that assumption had been. "I woke up feeling like ten pounds of trash in a 3 pound sack," he says. "I felt horrible."[26]

Several days passed, and Duvall's condition worsened. He writes: "I couldn't hide it anymore. I was sick and I knew it. My temperature was 104.3 and I felt horrible. . . . I have had the normal flu before but I knew that this was different." Duvall's health was deteriorating at an alarming pace. He reached the point where he could not breathe and was panting, fighting for air. When he starting spitting up blood, he became frightened: "After the bloody mucus began, I knew I was dying. It wasn't a fast dying, but I knew it was coming."[27]

Overcoming Illness

Duvall's parents called 911, and an ambulance rushed to his home to pick him up. At the hospital they were told that the situation was extremely grave. Duvall's immune system was all but destroyed, and his lungs were "packed concrete tight with bloody mucus." His only chance of survival was to be airlifted by helicopter to a larger hospital in Little Rock, Arkansas. Upon his arrival doctors found that his bone marrow was dying and his kidneys and liver were shutting down. For the next 12 days, Duvall lay in a medically induced coma, hooked up to a ventilator because he could not breathe on his own, fighting for his life. On three separate occa-

> " **Although seasonal influenza strikes like clockwork during the winter months, the same is not true of flu strains that lead to pandemics.** "

sions he went into cardiac arrest, and after the third time it looked like he was not going to make it. "This one was really bad," he says. "They called in all the family because they were sure I was a goner."[28]

In spite of the odds against him, however, Duvall survived his horrific battle with H1N1 influenza. When he finally woke up, he was extremely weak and fragile; he had lost 36 pounds (16kg). The first time he stood on his own was a monumental undertaking, as he explains: "It was harder than any sprint, workout, or football game I have ever experienced." Also excruciatingly difficult for Duvall was that he had to enter rehabilitation and "relearn how to live,"[29] including learning how to eat and drink all over again. Although he was relieved to be alive, he could not help becoming frustrated and depressed, as well as extremely homesick.

When Duvall was finally released from rehabilitation, he was elated. After more than a month of battling the worst disease of his life, he was more than ready to go home and get back to living a normal life. He found himself filled with a renewed sense of hope and purpose, as he writes: "After going through that, I know I can do anything."[30]

Sobering Realities

While it is true that most people who are infected with influenza recover without any lasting problems, it is a disease that can be life-threatening. Influenza viruses home in on the respiratory system, attacking cells with a vengeance and potentially causing serious damage. Many people still do not view influenza as a threat, believing that they and their families are not at risk. But those who have been stricken with the disease are the first to say that influenza should never, ever be taken lightly.

Primary Source Quotes*

What Is Influenza?

❝There are three types of influenza viruses, classified as A, B, or C, based on their protein composition. Public health experts are most concerned with type A.❞

—Infectious Diseases Society of America, "What Is Seasonal Influenza?" 2009. https://idsociety.org.

The Infectious Diseases Society seeks to improve public health through education, research, and prevention relating to infectious diseases.

❝A bird flu strain named H5N1 raised the concern of a new influenza pandemic after it emerged in Asia in the 1990s, but it has not changed into a form that spreads easily between people—yet.❞

—Terence Stephenson, *Swine Flu/H1N1: The Facts*. London: Jessica Kingsley, 2009.

Stephenson is a pediatrician and president of the Royal College of Paediatrics and Child Health in the United Kingdom.

* Editor's Note: While the definition of a primary source can be narrowly or broadly defined, for the purposes of Compact Research, a primary source consists of: 1) results of original research presented by an organization or researcher; 2) eyewitness accounts of events, personal experience, or work experience; 3) first-person editorials offering pundits' opinions; 4) government officials presenting political plans and/or policies; 5) representatives of organizations presenting testimony or policy.

Primary Source Quotes

> 66 Amazingly, influenza, the virus and the clinical syndrome that has existed for centuries and has been the subject of much medical and scientific research, still causes significant grief for humankind. 99

—Roni K. Devlin, *Influenza*. Westport, CT: Greenwood, 2008.

Devlin is a physician who specializes in infectious disease.

> 66 Differentiating a cold from the flu by symptoms alone can sometimes be difficult or impossible, but in general, people with the flu get sick more suddenly, look much sicker, and feel much weaker than if the ailment were a common cold. 99

—Steven Fine, "Flu in Adults," WebMD, February 4, 2010. www.emedicinehealth.com.

Fine is an assistant professor in the infectious disease division at the University of Rochester School of Medicine in New York.

> 66 For healthy children and adults, influenza is typically a moderately severe illness. Most people are back on their feet within a week. 99

—American Lung Association, "Influenza," 2010. www.lungusa.org.

The mission of the American Lung Association is to save lives by improving lung health and preventing lung disease.

> 66 Influenza ('the flu'), a highly contagious viral infection of the nose, throat and lungs, is one of the most severe illnesses of the winter season. 99

—National Foundation for Infectious Diseases, "Influenza: Fact Sheet," July 2008. www.nfid.org.

The National Foundation for Infectious Diseases is dedicated to educating the public and health-care professionals about the causes, treatment, and prevention of infectious diseases.

❝ Anyone can get influenza, but infection rates are highest among children. ❞

—Childhood Influenza Immunization Coalition, "Seasonal Flu Facts," 2009. www.preventchildhoodinfluenza.org.

The Childhood Influenza Immunization Coalition seeks to protect children's health by improving low influenza immunization rates.

❝ Influenza, commonly called the flu, is not the same as the stomach viruses that cause diarrhea and vomiting. ❞

—Mayo Clinic, "Influenza (Flu)," September 11, 2009. www.mayoclinic.com.

The Mayo Clinic is a world-renowned medical facility headquartered in Rochester, Minnesota.

What Is Influenza?

- The March of Dimes states that **5 to 20 percent** of Americans get influenza every year.

- Influenza viruses are **RNA-based**, meaning they have ribonucleic acid as their genetic base.

- According to the U.S. Department of Health and Human Services, children are **1.5 to 3 times more likely than adults** to get influenza.

- The Centers for Disease Control and Prevention states that 3 influenza A subtypes are circulating widely among humans worldwide: **H1N1, H1N2, and H3N2.**

- Most people who get influenza recover in less than **two weeks**.

- Since influenza is a viral rather than bacterial disease, **antibiotics have no effect** on it and should not be prescribed for treating it.

- St. Jude Children's Research Hospital states that about **50 percent** of those who are infected with influenza have no symptoms but are still contagious.

- Wild and domesticated **birds** can carry a wide range of flu viruses, but most do not infect humans.

- According to the Centers for Disease Control and Prevention, during the past 26 flu seasons in the Northern Hemisphere, the month with the heaviest influenza activity was **February** (12 seasons), followed by January (5 seasons), December and March (4 seasons each), and November (1 season).

Influenza Basics

Influenza, more commonly known as the flu, is a highly contagious respiratory illness. Although it usually causes mild to severe illness, it can be deadly. According to the Centers for Disease Control and Prevention, each year in the United States approximately 5 to 20 percent of the population gets the flu; more than 200,000 people are hospitalized with flu-related complications; and about 36,000 people die from flu-related causes. Influenza is characterized by certain common symptoms as well as established prevention and treatment strategies.

Symptoms	Fever; body aches and pains; headache; dry cough; sneezing; sore or dry throat; loss of appetite; runny nose; itchy or watery eyes; chills; fatigue
Emergency Warning Signs	**In adults:** difficulty breathing or shortness of breath; pain or pressure in the chest or abdomen; sudden dizziness; confusion; severe or persistent vomiting; flulike symptoms that improve but then return with fever and worse cough
	In children: fast breathing or working hard to breathe; bluish skin tone; not drinking fluids; not waking up or interacting; extreme irritability; fever with a rash; high fever; not eating; no tears when crying
Causes	Coming into contact with saliva from infected person who sneezes, coughs, or talks; touching an object that has germs, such as a telephone, doorknob, shopping cart, or keyboard
Treatment	Resting; drinking lots of water and other fluids; taking medicine to lower fever; taking antiviral medication prescribed by a doctor
Prevention	Getting yearly vaccines; washing hands frequently; avoiding sick people; avoiding crowded places; proper diet and sleep habits to maintain healthy immune system; if symptoms are apparent stay at home
High-Risk Groups	Children between 6 months and 4 years old; pregnant women; adults older than 55; people with long-term illness; people with impaired immune systems; health-care workers; childcare workers; residents or staff of nursing homes or long-term care facilities, schools, prisons, and dormitories

Sources: AOL Health, "Influenza," July 31, 2008. www.aolhealth.com; Centers for Disease Control and Prevention, "Know the Emergency Warning Signs," January 12, 2010. www.cdc.gov; Mayo Clinic, "Influenza," April 10, 2010.

The U.S. Flu Season

Winter is considered the primary flu season in the United States. Although seasonal flu outbreaks sometimes occur as early as October, flu activity usually peaks in January or later. Between the 1976–1977 flu season and the 2008–2009 flu season, February marked the month with the highest percentage of influenza cases in the United States, according to statistics compiled by the Centers for Disease Control and Prevention.

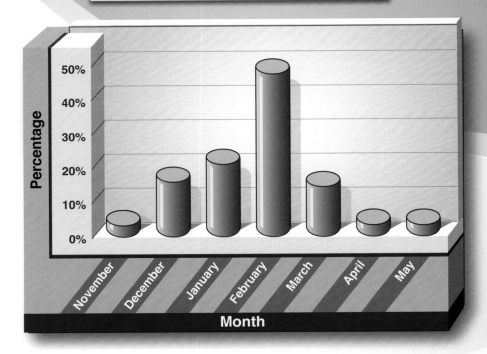

Peak Month of Influenza Activity

1976–1977 through 2008–2009 Seasons

Source: Centers for Disease Control and Prevention, "The Flu Season," January 27, 2009. www.cdc.gov.

- The National Foundation for Infectious Diseases states that estimated total hospitalization costs of a severe influenza epidemic are over **$3 billion.**

What Causes Influenza?

❝Influenza (also known as the flu) is very easy to 'catch' and is caused by a virus that spreads from person to person.❞

—Sanofi Pasteur, the world's largest company devoted exclusively to the manufacture of human vaccines.

❝You can't catch the flu by standing in the rain, wading through puddles, or sleeping in a drafty room. You can't catch the flu from a flu shot. And the common cold cannot worsen and transform into influenza.❞

—Delthia Ricks, a health and medical journalist and the author of *100 Questions & Answers About Influenza*.

Throughout history, the respiratory infection that is now called influenza was documented as a highly contagious, often deadly disease. As far back as 412 B.C., the Greek physician Hippocrates, who came to be known as the father of medicine, wrote about a flulike epidemic that was so severe it ravaged the Athenian army. Over the following centuries other noted physicians and scientists observed and wrote about the terrible illness that sickened and killed people year after year, but its cause remained a mystery. A breakthrough occurred in the late 1800s with discoveries about germs by the French chemist and biologist Louis Pasteur. Although his findings related specifically to bacteria, what Pasteur learned about germs paved the way toward broader scientific understanding of how germs cause disease. This also led to later discoveries about the link between viruses and influenza, although it was decades before anyone made that connection.

Quest for the Cause

Embracing the prevailing belief that bacteria caused influenza, German physician and bacteriologist Richard Friedrich Johannes Pfeiffer set out to prove it. He collected mucus samples from the noses of sick patients who were exhibiting flulike symptoms and discovered a commonality among the specimens: a small bacterium that he named *Bacillus influenzae*. In 1892 Pfeiffer published his findings in a report in which he claimed that the bacterium caused influenza. As researchers Jeffery K. Taubenberger, Johan V. Hultin, and David M. Morens write: "The scientific world was taken by storm; it seemed to many that Pfeiffer had taken all of the necessary steps to establish *Bacillus influenzae* . . . as the true aetiological agent [or cause] of influenza."[31]

Scientists continued to study influenza throughout the remainder of the 1800s and into the twentieth century. Although Pfeiffer's theory was still widely accepted, research was beginning to shed doubt on whether a bacterium was, in fact, the cause of influenza. One incident that contributed to the uncertainty occurred in 1918, when a ship carrying military troops arrived at a port in Philadelphia, Pennsylvania. Many of the soldiers were seriously ill with what appeared to be influenza, but mucus samples showed that very few were infected with bacteria. As Roni K. Devlin explains: "It was concluded that the epidemic at Camp Lewis was not caused by *Bacillus influenzae*, and it was further suggested that influenza might not be caused by a single bacterium at all." Devlin adds that autopsies performed on patients who had died from influenza showed that their lungs looked different from the lungs of patients known to have died from bacterial respiratory disease. She writes: "The suspicion for a possible viral agent as the cause for influenza could not be ignored."[32]

> **As far back as 412 B.C., the Greek physician Hippocrates, who came to be known as the father of medicine, wrote about a flulike epidemic that was so severe it ravaged the Athenian army.**

The turning point in the search for influenza's cause came in 1930.

American physician Richard E. Shope discovered that pigs had been infected with the flu, and he performed a series of experiments on the creatures. His findings led him to conclude that swine influenza was caused not by bacteria but by viruses, and he suggested that the same could be true of human influenza. Three years later, his theory was shown to be correct. British researchers Christopher Andrewes, Wilson Smith, and Patrick Laidlaw conducted experiments with ferrets and mice, and then performed tests on human volunteers who had influenza. The researchers confirmed that influenza in humans as well as other mammals was caused by viruses. Further studies reinforced this finding, as Devlin explains: "Other researchers collected field data, as well; patients sick in various outbreaks of influenza were routinely tested, and all were found to have the same virus."[33]

> **Because of a phenomenon known as antigenic drift, viral surface proteins continuously undergo changes over time, creating new virus strains that may not be recognized by the body's immune system.**

Drifting Viruses

A great deal has been learned about influenza since scientists correctly determined that it was caused by viruses. One important discovery was that more than one virus is involved in flu infection (classified as types A, B, and C) and that the viruses differ based on their varying protein compositions. It is also known that the type A virus, which is subdivided into groups based on the surface proteins hemagglutinin (H or HA) and neuraminidase (N or NA), is by far the most dangerous of all flu viruses. History has clearly shown that type A influenza strains result in the most widespread epidemics and the deadliest global pandemics.

Scientists have also discovered that influenza strains are not exactly the same from year to year. Because of a phenomenon known as antigenic drift, viral surface proteins continuously undergo changes over time, creating new virus strains that may not be recognized by the body's immune system. Delthia Ricks explains:

We can catch the flu more than once because antigenic drift causes flu viruses to change their H and N identity ever so slightly. The change is just enough to keep the human immune system a bit uncertain—questioning—whether this was the culprit it had seen the previous year, or whether it was another. Ongoing, subtle changes help explain why influenza viruses remain continuously infectious.[34]

Health officials worldwide closely monitor influenza outbreaks, scrutinizing viruses for changes that have occurred due to antigenic drift. In the United States the CDC collects data year-round and reports on flu activity each week from October through May. This allows the agency to determine when and where influenza activity is occurring and what types of influenza viruses are circulating. The CDC can detect changes in the influenza viruses that have been identified, track patterns of influenza-related illness, and measure the impact of influenza on the American population.

An important element in this ongoing influenza monitoring is to keep public health officials aware of what is happening with flu viruses in both hemispheres. For example, by tracking viruses that are circulating in the Southern Hemisphere, health officials can determine which strains are most likely to cause the flu the following winter in the Northern Hemisphere. Armed with this knowledge, scientists can develop vaccines that protect against the specific viruses that have been confirmed as being in circulation.

Shifting Viruses

In general the word *pandemic* is used to refer to an epidemic that spreads through a large geographic region and even the entire world. Pandemic influenza's severity, however, goes beyond how far and wide its infectious tentacles stretch. Unlike with seasonal influenza, flu viruses associated with pandemics have not merely evolved over time—they are newly formed viruses, possessing a genetic makeup that has not been known to exist before and is foreign to scientists. As Devlin writes: "The influenza subtypes that cause pandemic influenza do not arise by mutation from existing strains; thus, the origin of these viruses remains the focus of much research. The most accepted theory suggests that pandemic viruses arise from a cross of avian [bird] and human strains with drastic alterations in the viral HA and NA structures, a phenomenon known as antigenic shift."[35]

Antigenic shift represents abrupt, radical changes in type A influenza viruses that result from new hemagglutinin and/or hemagglutinin and neuraminidase proteins on the viral surfaces. Scientists say that this likely results from animal-to-human infection, followed by viral mutations that enable the new strain to be transmitted from human to human. Ricks offers another possible scenario: "Theoretically,

> " Unlike with seasonal influenza, flu viruses associated with pandemics have not merely evolved over time—they are newly formed viruses, possessing a genetic makeup that has not been known to exist before and is foreign to scientists. "

an animal virus can become easily transmissible if it jumps to a person who also happens to be infected with a seasonal flu strain. In that instance the animal and human flu strains might intermingle, causing the genetic material from the two viruses to undergo reassortment [which is] a mixing of genes."[36]

Ricks's reference to reassortment is applicable to the 2009 H1N1 influenza virus. In fact, according to a June 2009 report by an international team of researchers, H1N1 is a triple-reassortment virus, meaning it is composed of genes from three different sources: human, swine, and avian influenza type A viruses. This virus is typical of pandemic flu because of antigenic shift, as well as the speed with which it traveled throughout the world. By the time the World Health Organization learned of the April 2009 outbreak in Mexico and declared a global pandemic two months later, the disease was already well established and moving quickly.

Viruses Vying for Position

The ways that flu viruses change slightly through antigenic drift or shift into completely new viral strains that have never been seen before are important aspects of how viruses cause influenza. Another characteristic that is particularly interesting is that some viruses outcompete others. This refers to what happens when multiple flu strains are circulating at the same time and one overtakes the others to become the dominant strain. Pandemic flu viruses have historically outcompeted seasonal viruses, as a February 2010 *Washington Post* article explains: "The H1N1 family arrived in 1918 with the Spanish flu. In the 1957 pandemic, the new virus was in the HN2 family; it drove all H1N1 strains to extinction. In 1968, the new virus was an H3N2. It spelled the end of the H2N2 family, which disappeared. H1N1 returned in 1977, apparently the result of an accidental release from a laboratory in Russia or China."[37]

History is repeating itself with 2009 H1N1 influenza. Although the virus was most active in the Northern Hemisphere during the spring and summer of 2009, it was still circulating in the fall and into the winter, which is the typical flu season. The seasonal flu strains in circulation at the same time were H3N2, other forms of H1N1, and influenza B, and all were outcompeted by the 2009 H1N1 influenza strain. As French epidemiologist Cécile Viboud explains: "The seasonal virus is slowly driven to extinction."[38] This phenomenon is why very little seasonal flu activity was reported during the winter of 2009–2010: Most people who caught influenza were infected with the 2009 H1N1 strain. A strong indicator was the difference in age groups that were affected by the new virus. Nearly 90 percent of the influenza-related deaths were among people younger than 65, whereas the typical scenario with seasonal flu is that 90 percent of those who die are 65 and older.

> " According to scientists, a probable result of 2009 H1N1's outcompeting other flu strains is that it will become the new seasonal influenza. "

To better understand the concept of how seasonal and pandemic flu strains compete for biological superiority, researchers from the University of Maryland performed a study during the summer of 2009. Ferrets, which were chosen because their respiratory systems are very similar to that of humans, were each infected with 2009 H1N1 virus and either an

H1N1 or H3N2 seasonal virus. The creatures were sickened by both, but the H1N1 virus caused more severe disease.

The researchers also noted that the creatures only passed the new virus to uninfected ferrets and did not transmit either of the seasonal viruses. These findings clearly showed that the 2009 H1N1 virus was the dominant influenza strain, in terms of severity as well as contagion potential. As lead researcher Daniel Perez explains: "The H1N1 pandemic virus has a clear biological advantage over the two main seasonal flu strains. . . . I'm not surprised to find that the pandemic virus is more infectious, simply because it is new, so hosts haven't had a chance to build immunity yet. Meanwhile, the older strains encounter resistance from the hosts' immunity to them."[39]

According to scientists, a probable result of 2009 H1N1's outcompeting other flu strains is that it will become the new seasonal influenza. If so, it will emerge during regular flu season beginning in the fall of 2010 and will wane during the spring of 2011—the polar opposite of its behavior as a pandemic influenza virus. John Treanor, a professor of medicine, microbiology, and immunology at the University of Rochester Medical Center in New York, explains: "What most people are expecting is that [the new H1N1 strain] will supplant the older H1N1 viruses that were the previous seasonal strains and become the seasonal H1N1 virus. The most likely scenario would be that we would continue to see the descendants of pandemic H1N1 causing seasonal outbreaks of flu, with probably normal timing."[40]

More Work to Be Done

Numerous scientists throughout history have contributed to the current understanding of influenza's cause, including some who drew erroneous conclusions and others who proved that viruses are the culprits. Together they built a foundation of knowledge that is invaluable to today's researchers, whose focus now is to delve further into the reasons why flu viruses behave the way they do, from slight drifting to major genetic shifts that lead to pandemic flu strains. Despite all that is known, however, mysteries about influenza still remain. As more is learned about flu viruses, the disease may eventually be viewed as just another chapter in medical science history.

Primary Source Quotes*

What Causes Influenza?

> 66 The influenza virus is decidedly skillful in its ability to alter its surface proteins. 99

—Roni K. Devlin, *Influenza*. Westport, CT: Greenwood, 2008.

Devlin is a physician who specializes in infectious disease.

> 66 H1N1 flu, popularly known as swine flu, is a respiratory infection caused by an influenza virus first recognized in spring 2009. The new virus, which is officially called swine influenza A (H1N1), contains genetic material from human, swine and avian flu viruses. 99

—Mayo Clinic, "Swine Flu," September 30, 2009. www.mayoclinic.com.

The Mayo Clinic is a world-renowned medical facility headquartered in Rochester, Minnesota.

> 66 H1N1 flu is NOT caused by eating pork or pork products. H1N1 flu is not a foodborne disease, it is a respiratory disease. 99

—U.S. Department of Health and Human Services, "H1N1 (Swine Flu)," 2009. www.pandemicflu.gov.

The U.S. Department of Health and Human Services is the U.S. government's principal agency for protecting the health of all Americans.

* Editor's Note: While the definition of a primary source can be narrowly or broadly defined, for the purposes of Compact Research, a primary source consists of: 1) results of original research presented by an organization or researcher; 2) eyewitness accounts of events, personal experience, or work experience; 3) first-person editorials offering pundits' opinions; 4) government officials presenting political plans and/or policies; 5) representatives of organizations presenting testimony or policy.

Primary Source Quotes

"People who get infected with bird flu usually have direct contact with the infected birds or their waste products."

Charles Davis, "Flu (Influenza, Conventional and H1N1)," MedicineNet, October 29, 2009. www.medicinenet.com.

Davis is an emergency medicine physician from San Antonio, Texas.

"Influenza viruses . . . usually spread from person to person, though sometimes people become infected by touching something contaminated with the influenza virus and then touching their mouths or noses."

—American Lung Association, "Anyone Can Get Influenza," Faces of Influenza, 2010. www.facesofinfluenza.org.

The mission of the American Lung Association is to save lives by improving lung health and preventing lung disease.

"A person can be infected and spreading influenza for several days before his or her own symptoms start, so it is not always possible to avoid getting influenza just by avoiding people with symptoms."

—National Foundation for Infectious Diseases, "Influenza: Fact Sheet," July 2008. www.nfid.org.

The National Foundation for Infectious Diseases is dedicated to educating the public and health-care professionals about the causes, treatment, and prevention of infectious diseases.

"The flu shot cannot cause flu illness. The three influenza viruses contained in the flu vaccine are each inactivated (killed), which means they cannot cause infection."

—Centers for Disease Control and Prevention, *Influenza (Flu) Fact Sheet: Misconceptions About Influenza and Influenza Vaccine*, January 22, 2008. www.cdc.gov.

The Centers for Disease Control and Prevention seeks to promote health and quality of life by controlling disease, injury, and disability.

Facts and Illustrations

What Causes Influenza?

- Influenza is caused by a family of viruses known as *Orthomyxoviridae*, which infect vertebrate animals (those that have a bony spinal column, or backbone, and internal skeleton).

- Influenza virus type A viruses infect **humans, birds, pigs, horses, dogs**, and other animals.

- Influenza virus B usually infects only humans, although scientists have found that **seals and ferrets** are also susceptible.

- The most dangerous type of influenza virus is **type A**, which leads to all worldwide outbreaks known as pandemics.

- The Centers for Disease Control and Prevention states that **wild birds** are the natural host for all known subtypes of influenza A viruses, although direct human infection with avian influenza viruses seldom occurs.

- H1N1 flu viruses are **not transmitted by food** and cannot infect people who eat pork products.

- Influenza pandemics occur when a new strain of the **influenza virus is transmitted to humans from another animal species** such as pigs, chickens, and wild birds.

- According to the Centers for Disease Control and Prevention, there are substantial **genetic differences** between the influenza A subtypes that typically infect birds and those that infect both people and birds.

How Influenza Infection Occurs

Influenza spreads easily from person to person. When an infected person coughs or sneezes, droplets from the nose and throat are propelled through the air and deposited on the mouth or nose of anybody who is nearby. The virus can also be transmitted by touch. If a droplet lands on an object, and others touch that object and then touch their own nose and mouth before washing their hands, the virus will spread. Once a person comes in contact with the influenza virus, it is only a matter of time before it passes into the respiratory tract and illness occurs.

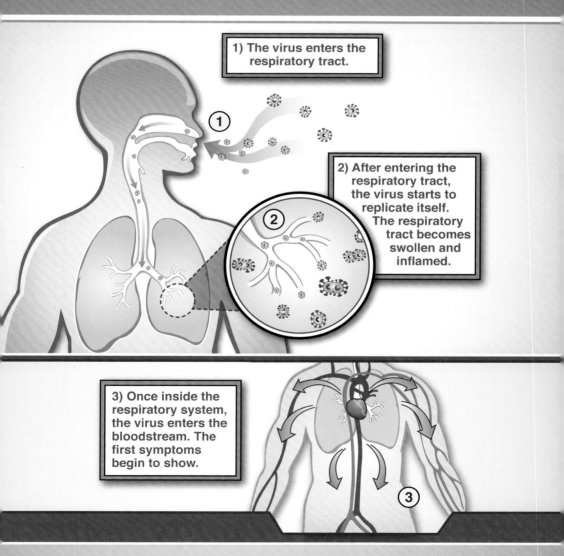

1) The virus enters the respiratory tract.

2) After entering the respiratory tract, the virus starts to replicate itself. The respiratory tract becomes swollen and inflamed.

3) Once inside the respiratory system, the virus enters the bloodstream. The first symptoms begin to show.

Source: HowStuffWorks.com, "How the Flu Works," by Stephanie Watson, 2010. www.howstuffworks.com.

A Global Survey of Avian Influenza

The avian influenza, or bird flu, virus occurs naturally in wild birds but usually does not infect humans. However, wild birds can spread the virus to domesticated birds such as chickens, ducks, and turkeys. Humans who come in contact with infected domesticated birds can contract avian flu. Although this does not occur often, it has occurred in Indonesia, Vietnam, and a few other countries.

Cumulative Number of Confirmed Human Cases of Avian Influenza A(H5N1) Reported to WHO

Cases | Deaths

Country	2003		2004		2005		2006		2007		2008		2009		2010		Total	
Azerbaijan	0	0	0	0	0	0	8	5	0	0	0	0	0	0	0	0	8	5
Bangladesh	0	0	0	0	0	0	0	0	0	0	1	0	0	0	0	0	1	0
Cambodia	0	0	0	0	4	4	2	2	1	1	1	0	1	0	1	1	10	8
China	1	1	0	0	8	5	13	8	5	3	4	4	7	4	0	0	38	25
Djibouti	0	0	0	0	0	0	1	0	0	0	0	0	0	0	0	0	1	0
Egypt	0	0	0	0	0	0	18	10	25	9	8	4	39	4	19	7	109	34
Indonesia	0	0	0	0	20	13	55	45	42	37	24	20	21	19	3	2	165	136
Iraq	0	0	0	0	0	0	3	2	0	0	0	0	0	0	0	0	3	2
Lao People's Democratic Republic	0	0	0	0	0	0	0	0	2	2	0	0	0	0	0	0	2	2
Myanmar	0	0	0	0	0	0	0	0	1	0	0	0	0	0	0	0	1	0
Nigeria	0	0	0	0	0	0	0	0	1	1	0	0	0	0	0	0	1	1
Pakistan	0	0	0	0	0	0	0	0	3	1	0	0	0	0	0	0	3	1
Thailand	0	0	17	12	5	2	3	3	0	0	0	0	0	0	0	0	25	17
Turkey	0	0	0	0	0	0	12	4	0	0	0	0	0	0	0	0	12	4
Vietnam	3	3	29	20	61	19	0	0	8	5	6	5	5	5	7	2	119	59
Total	4	4	46	32	98	43	115	79	88	59	44	33	73	32	30	12	498	294

Cold Versus Flu: The Symptoms Differ

Colds and flu are both respiratory illnesses and both are caused by viruses. Although the viruses that cause these illnesses are different, the symptoms can seem similar. In most cases, flu symptoms occur suddenly and include moderate to severe tiredness, chills, severe aches, and fever. Cold symptoms are usually less severe and often include a stuffy nose and productive cough. Colds may also be accompanied by minor aches and some tiredness.

Symptoms	Cold	Flu
Fever	Fever is rare with a cold.	Fever is usually present with the flu in up to 80% of all flu cases. A temperature of 100° F or higher for 3 to 4 days is associated with the flu.
Coughing	A hacking, productive (mucus-producing) cough is often present with a cold.	A nonproductive (non–mucus producing) cough is usually present with the flu (sometimes referred to as dry cough).
Aches	Slight body aches and pains can be part of a cold.	Severe aches and pains are common with the flu.
Stuffy Nose	Stuffy nose is commonly present with a cold and typically resolves spontaneously within a week.	Stuffy nose is not commonly present with the flu.
Chills	Chills are uncommon with a cold.	60% of people who have the flu experience chills.
Tiredness	Tiredness is fairly mild with a cold.	Tiredness is moderate to severe with the flu.
Sneezing	Sneezing is commonly present with a cold.	Sneezing is not common with the flu.
Sudden Symptoms	Cold symptoms tend to develop over a few days.	The flu has a rapid onset within 3–6 hours. The flu hits hard and includes sudden symptoms like high fever, aches, and pains.
Headache	A headache is fairly uncommon with a cold.	A headache is very common with the flu, present in 80% of flu cases.
Sore throat	Sore throat is commonly present with a cold.	Sore throat is not commonly present with the flu.
Chest Discomfort	Chest discomfort is mild to moderate with a cold.	Chest discomfort is often severe with the flu.

Source: Tamiflu, "Cold vs. Flu Tool," 2010. www.tamiflu.com.

- Through studies with influenza patients, researchers from Canada found that people infected with 2009 H1N1 influenza were **contagious longer** than those with seasonal flu, with some patients still harboring flu viruses as long as 16 days after symptoms appeared.

- Although scientists do not fully understand the genetic mutations that cause flu viruses to change continually, it is thought that human and animal strains **recombine to create new influenza strains.**

- Once people have been infected with a particular influenza virus (such as 2009 H1N1), their bodies develop **immune resistance** to that virus, making it unlikely that they would be infected with the identical flu virus again.

What Are the Public Health Risks of Influenza?

66**Without a doubt, influenza is considered a serious form of respiratory infection around the globe, in nations large and small, and even on remote islands. No region on Earth is immune to influenza.**99

—Delthia Ricks, a health and medical journalist and the author of *100 Questions & Answers About Influenza.*

66**Influenza pandemics, whether moderate or severe, are remarkable events because of the almost universal susceptibility of the world's population to infection.**99

—Margaret Chan, director general of the World Health Organization.

The most devastating influenza pandemic in history began in the fall of 1918, as World War I was coming to an end. In less than two years, the disease that was known as the Spanish flu swept across the world in a ferocious attack that claimed tens of millions of lives. Nearly a century has passed since the 1918 pandemic, and there are very few people today who were around during that time. But for those who are still alive, the haunting memories are burned deep into their minds and hearts, never to be forgotten.

Margaret Duchez is one of the few remaining survivors. Now 95 years old, Duchez was just a little girl when the deadly flu struck the town where she lived near Cleveland, Ohio. Fear permeated the entire community, with people terrified to walk to church, stroll around in the streets, or even go outside at all. Duchez says that her grandmother locked the door to ensure that she would stay in the house and not go out to play, fearing that she would be exposed to the virus. As the disease raged, the death toll rose at an unthinkable rate. Duchez recalls: "People were dying so fast in our parish, which was old St. Patrick's, they could not bury them fast enough."[41]

Could It Happen Today?

Remembering the 1918 Spanish flu pandemic is important not only because of its place in history, but also because a pandemic equal to or even worse than that one could potentially occur again. Roni K. Devlin writes: "Now, more than ever, an understanding of the events of that outbreak is necessary if humankind is to attempt to survive, or perhaps even prevent, another such pandemic."[42] And the risk is substantial. Since antigenic shift creates flu viruses that are foreign and completely unpredictable, there is no way for scientists to know which flu strains might emerge at any given time. Thus, a serious global pandemic seems inevitable, as Devlin explains: "It is considered fairly certain within the medical community that a significant, worldwide pandemic of influenza will occur sometime in the future, despite the current understanding of the virus and the ongoing attempts to control it. It has been postulated that the global mortality of such a pandemic could be as high as 62 million deaths."[43]

The 2009–2010 pandemic was nowhere near as grim as Devlin describes. But when the new H1N1 influenza strain started killing people in Mexico and then raced through other parts of the world, many health officials feared that it could become a public health disaster. This was a flu strain never before seen in humans, one that was virulent and extremely contagious. And because no vaccine had yet been developed to protect against it, fear grew. An August 2009 report to President Barack Obama by a council of science and technology advisors stressed the gravity of the situation. "Indeed," they wrote, "the 2009-H1N1 influenza is already responsible for significant morbidity and mortality worldwide—from its appearance in the spring, its continued circulation in the U.S. this summer, and its spread through many countries in the Southern Hemisphere during their winter season."[44]

Although the advisors stated that there was no way to predict the precise impact of H1N1 influenza, they provided a "plausible scenario"[45] of public health threats. These included up to 50 percent of Americans being infected, with more than half needing medical attention. As many as 1.8 million hospital admissions were projected, with 300,000 patients being sick enough to require care in intensive care units. The anticipated deaths ranged from 30,000 to 90,000, with the largest number of victims children and young adults.

A year after the World Health Organization declared the 2009 H1N1 flu pandemic, it was obvious that fears had been overblown and projections had exceeded reality. Children and young adults were indeed hardest hit by the disease, and the death rate among youth was significantly higher than seasonal influenza epidemics of the past. But the overall number of Americans sickened by H1N1 flu was much lower than predicted, as was the number of deaths. Still, health officials insist that the cautionary measures taken were warranted. As a May 19, 2010, *New England Journal of Medicine* article states: "Ultimately, the rate of death was lower than was initially predicted, but the numbers of H1N1 cases, hospitalizations, and deaths were nonetheless substantial, and the experience offers some lessons that may help us to prepare for future influenza outbreaks."[46]

> **Remembering the 1918 Spanish flu pandemic is important not only because of its place in history, but also because a pandemic equal to or even worse than that one could potentially occur again.**

When Birds Infect People

For years scientists have been concerned about flu viruses that are carried by wild birds. Millions of birds, including ducks, geese, and other waterfowl, harbor type A flu viruses in their intestinal tracts. Although they do not usually become sick, they can pass the viruses along to domestic birds, including chickens, ducks, and turkeys, as well as some other animals.

It was long believed that these viruses could not be passed from birds to humans, but that has proved to be incorrect. Even though it is extremely rare, bird-to-human transmission is possible—in fact, it is what led to the 1918 Spanish flu pandemic. A long-term, extensive study by influenza expert Jeffery K. Taubenberger and a team of researchers yielded the astonishing discovery that humans had caught the deadly virus directly from birds, as Delthia Ricks explains: "The pathogen apparently jumped the species barrier directly from birds to humans—an extraordinarily unusual occurrence."[47]

The Looming Threat of Avian Flu

The avian flu virus that is being closely watched by public health officials is H5N1, which was first identified in Scotland during the 1950s. Chickens were reportedly dying of a mysterious disease, and biologists concluded that the animals had been infected by wild birds carrying H5N1. Although the virus was known to be deadly to domestic birds such as poultry, it was not perceived as a threat to humans. That changed, however, in 1997.

Eighteen people in Hong Kong became infected with the H5N1 virus after direct contact with poultry, and six of them died. After other infections and deaths were reported throughout Asia and Africa, health officials considered H5N1 to be a grave threat to humans. As Ricks explains: "H5N1, which never before had infected humans, signaled the potential for a pandemic strain, one that might whip through human populations with unprecedented ferocity and speed."[48]

> " A year after the World Health Organization declared the 2009 H1N1 flu pandemic, it was obvious that fears had been overblown and projections had exceeded reality. "

Widespread human infection never materialized, and H5N1 has since been considered primarily an avian disease. Although the virus can be transmitted between birds and humans, it is not passed easily from human to human, as Terence Stephenson writes: "So far, person-to-person spread, if it has occurred, has done so with difficulty. In almost all cases, those infected have had extensive physical contact with infected birds."[49] The H5N1 virus is still considered a potential threat, though, because of its prolific presence among the world's birds, and especially because of how lethal it is for those infected with it. According to the World Health Organization, as of June 2010, 499 laboratory-confirmed cases of H5N1 have been reported, and of those, 295 people died—an unprecedented 60 percent mortality rate.

> **Even if research shows that H5N1 is incapable of being transmitted from person to person, that does not mean the virus no longer poses a threat.**

Even if research shows that H5N1 is incapable of being transmitted from person to person, that does not mean the virus no longer poses a threat. The possibility exists that the virus could genetically interact with a seasonal flu virus, thus creating a new hybrid strain through antigenic shift. This was demonstrated in a study that was published in February 2010. A team of researchers from the University of Wisconsin–Madison used genes from the H3N2 seasonal flu virus to convert the avian H5N1 virus into a highly pathogenic (infectious) virus in mice.

Although the experiment was considered a success, the outcome was worrisome to the scientists because of what it could mean for a potential avian influenza pandemic. Virologist Yoshihiro Kawaoka explains: "With the new pandemic H1N1 virus, people sort of forgot about H5N1 avian influenza. But the reality is that H5N1 avian virus is still out there. Our data suggests that it is possible there may be reassortment between H5 and pandemic H1N1 that can create a more pathogenic H5N1 virus."[50]

Dangerous Effects

Statistics have shown that most people who are infected with influenza, including seasonal types and 2009 H1N1, recover within a few weeks with no lasting problems. But there are also serious health risks associated with the disease, the most common of which is viral or bacterial pneumonia. Together, pneumonia and influenza represent the sixth leading cause of death in the United States. An August 2009 article in *New Scientist* describes the deadly aspects of influenza: "It is not a nice way to die. As the virus spreads through your lungs, your immune system goes into overdrive. Your lungs become leaky and fill with fluid. Your lips and nails, then your skin, turn blue as you struggle to get enough oxygen. Basically, you drown. Flu can kill in other ways, too, from rendering you vulnerable to bacterial infections to triggering heart attacks."[51]

Influenza also poses a significant threat for pregnant women, and 2009 H1N1 has proved to be especially risky. According to the CDC, pregnant women are seven times more likely to be hospitalized with H1N1 influenza than the general population and four times more likely to die from it. Margaret Chan, director general of the World Health Organization, reinforces the CDC warning: "Without question, pregnant women are at increased risk of complications. This heightened risk takes on added importance for a virus, like this one, that preferentially infects younger age groups."[52]

> **According to the CDC, pregnant women are seven times more likely to be hospitalized with H1N1 influenza than the general population and four times more likely to die from it.**

A study that was published in March 2010 showed that women who contracted H1N1 influenza were 13 times more likely to become critically ill if they were pregnant. Researchers from Australia and New Zealand examined 64 women who were admitted to hospital intensive care units with H1N1, all of whom were either pregnant or had recently given birth. Of those, 44 had to be put on ventilators to assist with breathing, and 7 of the women died. According to lead researcher Ian Seppelt, even though a mortality rate of 11 percent may seem low when compared with usual cases of respiratory failure among intensive care patients, "a maternal mortality of 11 percent is high when compared with any other obstetric condition."[53]

One woman who came dangerously close to becoming a mortality statistic is Karin McHugh. She was nine months pregnant in July 2009 when she suddenly began wheezing and coughing. After a visit to her doctor, McHugh was diagnosed with bronchitis and given an inhaler. A few days later she developed a fever and felt so exhausted that she could not even get out of bed. Certain that something was very wrong, her husband rushed her to the hospital.

When X-rays showed that McHugh's lungs were filled with fluid, she was diagnosed with pneumonia and placed on a ventilator. Tests later showed that she had been infected with H1N1—and as it turned out, she had one of the worst cases of H1N1 influenza that the doctors had ever seen. Her organs began shutting down, and because her baby was in danger of dying, an emergency cesarean section was performed. McHugh delivered a healthy baby boy, but she did not see him because she was in a medically induced coma. For the next seven weeks she lay in a hospital bed, breathing with the aid of a ventilator and fighting for her life.

McHugh survived, however, and saw her son for the first time when he was nearly two months old. She was deeply saddened by the loss of so much time with him, but relieved to be alive. "I'm very fortunate," she says. "My outcome is a miracle."[54]

Remaining Vigilant

Influenza poses a significant threat to people in every country of the world. Scientists have scrutinized the pandemic of 1918, as well as analyzed and documented the behavior of innumerable flu viruses. Yet there is still much uncertainty, as Devlin writes: "Although medical advances have certainly been made since 1918, today's population is increasingly at risk for a great pandemic from a disease such as influenza."[55] To help mitigate that risk and protect people from the deadly effects of flu viruses, scientific research will continue to focus on influenza. Hopefully, this will yield discoveries that reduce the risk or erase it altogether.

What Are the Public Health Risks of Influenza?

66 We estimate that the rate of death in young people [from H1N1 influenza] is probably five times higher than what we would typically see with seasonal influenza. 99

—Anne Schuchat, a participant in "CDC 2009 H1N1 Flu Media Briefing," Centers for Disease Control and Prevention Press Briefing Transcript, March 29, 2010. www.cdc.gov.

Schuchat is assistant U.S. surgeon general.

66 There is no problem with the H1N1 virus. It's no different from any other seasonal virus. 99

—Tom Jefferson, interviewed by Maryann Napoli, "Why the Swine Flu Isn't a Major Threat," Center for Medical Consumers, September 24, 2009. http://medicalconsumers.org.

Jefferson is a physician and epidemiologist based in Rome, Italy.

* Editor's Note: While the definition of a primary source can be narrowly or broadly defined, for the purposes of Compact Research, a primary source consists of: 1) results of original research presented by an organization or researcher; 2) eyewitness accounts of events, personal experience, or work experience; 3) first-person editorials offering pundits' opinions; 4) government officials presenting political plans and/or policies; 5) representatives of organizations presenting testimony or policy.

> 66 The influenza pandemic of 1918 may be the most dramatic and devastating medical event that has ever occurred in history. 99

—Roni K. Devlin, *Influenza*. Westport, CT: Greenwood, 2008.

Devlin is a physician who specializes in infectious disease.

> 66 At present, H1N1 flu is no worse than ordinary flu, but it is likely that many more people will be infected than in an average winter season. So more people will be ill and therefore more people will die than in a non-pandemic year. 99

—Terence Stephenson, *Swine Flu/H1N1: The Facts*. London: Jessica Kingsley, 2009.

Stephenson is a pediatrician and president of the Royal College of Paediatrics and Child Health in the United Kingdom.

> 66 The very young, the very old, and those in the high-risk groups are at risk for complications, including hospitalization. Some people may die from flu. 99

—Steven Fine, "Flu in Adults," WebMD, February 4, 2010. www.emedicinehealth.com.

Fine is an assistant professor in the infectious disease division at the University of Rochester School of Medicine in New York.

> 66 Type C infection usually causes either a very mild respiratory illness or no symptoms at all; it does not cause epidemics and does not have the severe public-health impact of influenza types A and B. 99

—Charles Davis, "Flu (Influenza, Conventional and H1N1)," MedicineNet, October 29, 2009. www.medicinenet.com.

Davis is an emergency medicine physician from San Antonio, Texas.

❝Seasonal influenza spreads easily and can sweep through schools, nursing homes or businesses and towns.❞

—World Health Organization, "Influenza (Seasonal)," April 2009. www.who.int.

The World Health Organization is the directing and coordinating authority for health within the United Nations system.

❝Unlike most other common respiratory and stomach infections that are often called 'the flu,' influenza can cause more severe illness and can result in complications leading to hospitalization and death, especially among the elderly.❞

—National Foundation for Infectious Diseases, "Influenza: Fact Sheet," July 2008. www.nfid.org.

The National Foundation for Infectious Diseases is dedicated to educating the public and health-care professionals about the causes, treatment, and prevention of infectious diseases.

❝Infants and toddlers are hospitalized with influenza infection at high rates. These hospitalization rates are comparable or higher than the influenza-related hospitalization rates of any other group, including elderly persons.❞

—Childhood Influenza Immunization Coalition, *Improving Childhood Influenza Immunization Rates to Protect Our Nation's Children*, October 2008. www.preventchildhoodinfluenza.org.

The Childhood Influenza Immunization Coalition seeks to protect children's health by improving low influenza immunization rates.

What Are the Public Health Risks of Influenza?

- According to a 2009 poll by *USA Today*, **62 percent** of respondents believed it was unlikely that they or a family member would get sick from H1N1 influenza.

- The Centers for Disease Control and Prevention states that from April 2009 through April 10, 2010, reported cases of H1N1 influenza in the United States ranged from **43 million to 89 million**, and deaths ranged from **8,870 to 18,300**.

- In June 2009 the World Health Organization declared H1N1 influenza to be the **first pandemic of the twenty-first century**, and in October 2009 President Barack Obama declared it a national emergency.

- The World Health Organization states that as of May 9, 2010, **214 countries** had reported outbreaks of H1N1 influenza.

- The World Health Organization states that annual influenza epidemics worldwide result in about **3 million to 5 million** cases of severe illness and **250,000 to 500,000 deaths**.

- Medicare states that influenza is the **sixth leading cause** of death among American adults.

- According to the American Lung Association, influenza and pneumonia combined are the **fourth leading cause of death** among all American women.

The Dramatic Rise of H1N1 Between 2009 and 2010

May 2009 was still early in the H1N1 pandemic. By that time, confirmed cases were mostly limited to North America, Western Europe, and China with Mexico experiencing the highest number of deaths. A year later, in May 2010, H1N1 had spread to nearly all parts of the world. Confirmed deaths from H1N1 also climbed on a global scale.

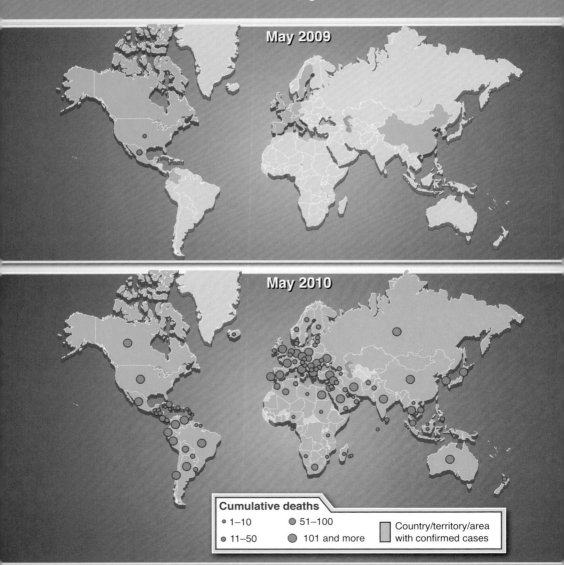

May 2009

May 2010

Cumulative deaths

- 1–10
- 11–50
- 51–100
- 101 and more

☐ Country/territory/area with confirmed cases

Sources: World Health Organization, "Pandemic (H1N1) 2009 Laboratory Confirmed Cases and Number of Deaths as Reported to WHO," May 2009. www.who.int; WHO, "Pandemic (H1N1) 2009: Countries, Territories and Areas with Lab Confirmed and Number of Deaths as Reported to WHO," May 16, 2010. www.who.int.

U.S. Influenza Hospitalizations and Deaths, 2009–2010

Between August 30, 2009 and April 3, 2010, a total of 41,914 laboratory-confirmed influenza-related hospitalizations and 2,125 laboratory-confirmed influenza-related deaths were reported to the Centers for Disease Control and Prevention. These numbers include all types of influenza, not just those associated with 2009 H1N1. The peak for influenza-related hospitalizations and deaths during this reporting period came during the forty-third and forty-fourth weeks.

Laboratory-Confirmed Influenza-Related Hospitalizations and Deaths

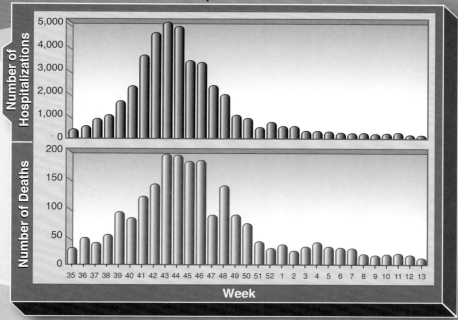

Source: Centers for Disease Control and Prevention, "FluView: 2009–2010 Influenza Season Week 19 Ending May 15, 2010," May 2010. www.cdc.gov.

• Four Gallup polls conducted from October 2009 to January 2010 found that **Hispanic Americans** were consistently more than twice as likely to report having influenza than Caucasians, African Americans, and Asian Americans.

- Those who are over the age of **65, people of any age with chronic medical conditions, pregnant women, and young children** are most likely to suffer from complications of influenza such as pneumonia, bronchitis, sinus infections, and ear infections.

- According to the U.S. Department of Health and Human Services, deaths of older adults account for more than **90 percent** of deaths attributed to influenza and pneumonia.

- According to the National Center for Health Statistics, children with influenza miss an estimated **38 million school days** each year.

Can Influenza Outbreaks Be Prevented?

> **We must also be aware that revealing the biology of a pandemic that occurred nearly 90 years ago is not just a historical exercise. It may well help us prepare for, and even prevent, the emergence of new pandemics in the 21st century and beyond.**
>
> — Jeffery K. Taubenberger, Johan V. Hultin, and David M. Morens, researchers with the National Institute of Allergy and Infectious Diseases.

> **For now, the best tools to mitigate influenza infection are tried-and-true—vaccination, social distancing, hand washing, and common sense.**
>
> —David M. Weinstock, assistant professor at Harvard Medical School, and Gianna Zuccotti, infectious disease physician in New York City.

On April 23, 2009, Mexican officials contacted the World Health Organization about a serious public health issue. Several hundred people had been sickened by a mysterious viral illness, and at least 20 had died. Canadian researchers had tested the virus and determined that it was H1N1, at the time referred to as swine flu. By the time it was identified, the situation in Mexico had become dire and was rapidly growing worse. In an effort to stop the spread of the disease, Mexican president Felipe Calderón decided that drastic measures were in order. He declared a state of emergency and ordered immediate mass closures of schools, nurseries, universities, libraries, theaters, and museums in Mexico City. Normally packed soccer stadiums were empty, restaurants only filled takeout orders, and even Sunday mass was canceled at churches.

Futile Attempts to Stop H1N1

As a result of Calderón's directive, an estimated 35,000 public venues were shut down and one of the most populous cities in the world soon resembled a ghost town. Deputy foreign minister Lourdes Aranda explains: "The Mexican way of life came to a halt. Imagine, in a colourful, bustling city, people had to stay home for days." Aranda says that it was a complete standstill in Mexico City, with only police and other emergency personnel being free to move about. No more than six people were allowed to be in elevators at one time, and press conferences about the epidemic were held out in the open rather than inside. "There were no cinemas, no bars, no parties," Aranda says. "The president came on TV and told the people to stay home. He meant everyone—rich or poor."[56]

> **Despite frantic efforts to curtail the spread of influenza, including other countries canceling flights to and from Mexico, the H1N1 virus was on the move and spreading at a rapid pace.**

Calderón's executive order was in effect for a month and a half. Although his decision was controversial, Aranda is of the opinion that it was essential under the circumstances. "I think what Mexico did was very responsible in terms of global health," she says. "We took the blow economically but it was the best thing to do."[57] Her reference to an economic "blow" is a major reason why not everyone agrees with such extreme measures during an influenza outbreak. Bringing business, commerce, entertainment, and travel to a sudden halt incurs a tremendous economic cost, and whether it pays off in terms of saving human lives is questionable.

Another question is whether such measures actually work—and it would appear that Calderón's efforts did not. Despite frantic efforts to curtail the spread of influenza, including other countries canceling flights to and from Mexico, the H1N1 virus was on the move and spreading at a rapid pace. The virus crept over the Mexican border and into the United States, and then moved on from there. Within five months of the initial outbreak in Mexico, at least 140 countries were reporting H1N1 illnesses, and the cases continued to rise day by day. As Delthia Ricks notes, this is indicative of pandemic influenza's ability to "spread around the world with frightening speed."[58]

Personal Responsibility for Health

As news about the new H1N1 flu strain became common knowledge, people started taking precautionary measures to protect themselves. Suddenly, commonsense efforts such as hand washing were on everyone's mind as the public learned how easily and quickly flu viruses can be spread from person to person. Hand sanitizers flew off store shelves as people purchased them by the boxful, and this increased demand led to skyrocketing sales. According to data by the consumer research firm Nielsen, in the 24 weeks prior to October 3, 2009, sales of hand sanitizers totaled $118.4 million—a 70.5 percent jump over the same period during 2008. Health officials have noted that a renewed public commitment to personal cleanliness, as simple as it may seem, can have a substantial impact on stopping the spread of influenza.

A report published in the May 19, 2010, issue of the *New England Journal of Medicine* was a strong indicator of precautions Americans are taking to guard against influenza infection. A team of researchers performed a comprehensive review of 20 national polls conducted between April 2009 and January 2010, with the goal of determining whether people had adopted specific behaviors during the H1N1 flu pandemic when a vaccine was not yet available. The authors write: "In the pandemic's first weeks, almost two thirds of Americans (59 to 67%) said that they or someone in their family had begun to wash their hands or clean them with

> " It is possible that H1N1 influenza would not have sickened so many people and would have claimed fewer lives if a vaccine had been available when the illness first emerged in Mexico. "

> **No matter how aggressively public health officials promote the importance of the flu vaccine or how hard they try to convince the public that vaccinations are safe, some people remain skeptical.**

sanitizer more frequently."[59] A separate study by researchers from China, published in June 2010, yielded similar findings. It showed that 47 percent of respondents washed their hands more frequently than usual, sometimes as often as 10 times per day.

The Chinese researchers also found that 89 percent of respondents wore face masks when exhibiting flu-like symptoms and 21.5 percent wore them on a regular basis while in public areas. The issue of face masks has been a topic of interest among public health officials. The practice was common in Mexico after H1N1 influenza began to spread, as well as other cities throughout the world. And while it is important for health-care professionals to wear the masks in order to help prevent the spread of infection, whether the general public should also wear them is an issue of some controversy. As Terence Stephenson writes:

> In healthcare settings, studies suggest that the use of masks could reduce the transmission of influenza. In the community, however, the benefits of wearing masks has not been established, especially in open areas, as opposed to enclosed spaces while in close contact with a person with influenza-like symptoms. Therefore, I would not recommend that healthy people wear facemasks to go about their everyday business.[60]

The Flu Vaccine

It is possible that H1N1 influenza would not have sickened so many people and would have claimed fewer lives if a vaccine had been available when the illness first emerged in Mexico. This was not possible, however, because there was no way for scientists to develop a vaccine without knowing exactly which virus they were dealing with. As with all pandemic flu viruses, the one that causes H1N1 influenza was newly formed and previously unknown. Only after its precise genetic makeup had been identified could development of a vaccine get underway.

Yet even when scientists had all the facts about the H1N1 virus and were certain what needed to be contained in the vaccine, a monumental task lay ahead, and time was ticking away—thus, they were under immense pressure to produce a vaccine faster than one had ever been made before. Health journalist Steve Sternberg writes:

> The challenges seemed almost overwhelming . . . grow out a strain [of H1N1 virus] that could be used to make a vaccine; determine who needs protection most; get the seed-strain to drug firms capable of making vaccine; test it for safety, effectiveness and dosing; churn out millions of doses; create, from scratch, mass vaccination programs; ramp up hospital surge capacity; get antiviral drugs to the people who need them most; and inform the public without sowing misinformation and panic.[61]

Even when the new H1N1 vaccine became available, initial supplies fell short of demand, and drug manufacturers were scrambling to produce ample quantities. Ironically, the very fact that the vaccine was developed and produced so quickly made the public skeptical, and many refused to be vaccinated because they were not confident it was safe. This concern is not unique to the H1N1 vaccine, however. For years some people have been afraid of flu shots because they believed they could cause influenza, which is a myth. Flu vaccines are made with inactivated viral particles rather than live, active viruses. And although the nasal spray vaccine known as FluMist is composed of live viruses, they are attenuated, meaning they have been extraordinarily weakened, and cannot cause the flu.

Yet no matter how aggressively public health officials promote the importance of the flu vaccine or how hard they try to convince the public that vaccinations are safe, some people remain skeptical. This is true not only of adults rejecting flu shots for themselves, but also parents refusing to have their children vaccinated. Jill Matthews, who is a public health professional from Michigan, has seen this happen many times, and she finds it not only frustrating but frightening. She explains:

I have worked in the public health field for more than 20 years, and in that time I have become very familiar with influenza and other infectious diseases. I've attended a number of autopsies including many performed on young children—and I will tell you that I have never, not even once, attended an autopsy for a child who died because of being vaccinated. But the sad reality is, I *have* attended a number of autopsies for children who were not vaccinated, and died needlessly because of a disease that could have been prevented. I'd give anything if I could get that message to every single parent who decides against vaccinating because they are taking a deadly chance with their child's life.[62]

The Promise of Antivirals

Many physicians prescribe antiviral medications such as Tamiflu to patients suffering from influenza. These drugs, which come in pill, liquid, or inhaled form, do not cure influenza, as there is no cure, nor do they get rid of flu viruses. They work by attacking viral enzymes, deactivating them so that the viruses lose the capability to reproduce and spread. As the CDC states: "While CDC recommends a yearly seasonal flu vaccine as the first and most important step in protecting against seasonal flu, antiviral drugs are a second line of defense against the flu."[63] People who take antiviral medications often feel better because their symptoms become less severe. Another benefit of antivirals is that they can shorten the time someone is sick with influenza by a day or two.

> **Influenza has been a known scourge of civilization for as long as historical documents have been kept.**

One drawback of antiviral medications is that they are only effective if started within 24 to 48 hours of becoming infected. Thus, if people wait too long before seeking medical attention (which is often the case), antiviral drugs will do them no good. In June 2010 a Wisconsin company called FluGen announced a breakthrough development that may overcome the limited window of time, as well as more effectively treat influenza. FluGen has created a new antiviral drug that is effective for several days after flu symptoms appear. According to a June 2010 article in *Wisconsin Business*, FluGen officials claim that the drug will "stop viruses in their tracks" after someone has been infected. As the article explains: "The peptide, a short chain of amino acids, blocks entry of the influenza virus into human cells, thus preventing the spread of the viral genetic code into healthy cells. By interrupting this transmission, the body's own immune system is able to respond more effectively."[64] The new antiviral drug is expected to be available for human clinical trials in 2011 or 2012 and available commercially in less than five years.

Can Influenza Be Stopped?

Influenza has been a known scourge of civilization for as long as historical documents have been kept. It has swept through cities, states, countries, and even entire continents, leaving a trail of sickness and death in its wake. For scientists, influenza is a source of interest, fear, fascination, frustration, and opportunity. A vast amount of information has been gained about influenza throughout the centuries as physicians, researchers, and noted scholars have studied it.

Yet so much more needs to be learned, and undoubtedly will be learned, in the coming years. In her role as an infectious disease physician, Roni K. Devlin has seen the terrible effects of influenza firsthand, and she is hopeful about scientific discoveries that are yet to come. As she writes: "Influenza is a fascinating virus, and the disease it causes will continue to be the focus of much discussion, research, and scholarly activity. Perhaps . . . a full understanding of the virus' role throughout the world's history will help with answers to questions about the implications of the disease for the future."[65]

Can Influenza Outbreaks Be Prevented?

❝Vaccination against influenza remains the best weapon available to fight the seasonal illness that has plagued humankind for centuries.❞

—Roni K. Devlin, *Influenza*. Westport, CT: Greenwood, 2008.

Devlin is a physician who specializes in infectious disease.

❝There is no evidence whatsoever that seasonal influenza vaccines have any effect, especially in the elderly and young children. No evidence of reduced [number of] cases, deaths, complications.❞

—Tom Jefferson, interviewed by Maryann Napoli, "Why the Swine Flu Isn't a Major Threat," Center for Medical Consumers, September 24, 2009. http://medicalconsumers.org.

Jefferson is a physician and epidemiologist based in Rome, Italy.

Bracketed quotes indicate conflicting positions.

* Editor's Note: While the definition of a primary source can be narrowly or broadly defined, for the purposes of Compact Research, a primary source consists of: 1) results of original research presented by an organization or researcher; 2) eyewitness accounts of events, personal experience, or work experience; 3) first-person editorials offering pundits' opinions; 4) government officials presenting political plans and/or policies; 5) representatives of organizations presenting testimony or policy.

❝It may seem very simple and low-tech, but good personal health and hygiene habits are the essence of preventing transmission of the [influenza] virus.❞

—Terence Stephenson, *Swine Flu/H1N1: The Facts.* London: Jessica Kingsley, 2009.

Stephenson is a pediatrician and president of the Royal College of Paediatrics and Child Health in the United Kingdom.

❝Undoubtedly, new surprises await in the perpetual struggle with influenza as one thing is certain—the organism will continue to evolve.❞

—David M. Weinstock and Gianna Zuccotti, "The Evolution of Influenza Resistance and Treatment," *Journal of the American Medical Association*, March 11, 2009. http://jama.ama-assn.org.

Weinstock is an assistant professor at Harvard Medical School and Zuccotti is an infectious disease physician in New York City.

❝Vaccinating people against the flu would be much simpler if only one shot was needed, with perhaps a booster dose every few years. Even better would be manufacturing this new kind of flu shot in a cell culture or by way of some other advanced technique. . . . Remarkably, scientists are on the trail of such a goal.❞

—Delthia Ricks, *100 Questions & Answers About Influenza.* Sudbury, MA: Jones and Bartlett, 2009.

Ricks is a journalist and author who specializes in topics related to health and medicine.

❝Vaccination and early treatment with antiviral medications are very important for healthcare personnel at higher risk for influenza complications because they can prevent hospitalizations and deaths.❞

—Centers for Disease Control and Prevention, "Interim Guidance on Infection Control Measures for 2009 H1N1 Influenza in Healthcare Settings, Including Protection of Healthcare Personnel," May 3, 2010. www.cdc.gov.

The Centers for Disease Control and Prevention seeks to promote health and quality of life by controlling disease, injury, and disability.

66 **IDSA [Infectious Diseases Society of America] strongly believes that much work remains ahead of us, and overall responses to seasonal influenza and pandemic preparedness must be closely interrelated.** 99

—Infectious Diseases Society of America, "Pandemic and Seasonal Influenza," 2009. www.idsociety.org.

The Infectious Diseases Society of America's purpose is to improve the health of individuals and communities through education, research, and prevention relating to infectious diseases.

66 **While vaccination is the primary means of preventing influenza infection, antiviral medications may be used effectively in certain situations, such as during institutional outbreaks.** 99

—National Foundation for Infectious Diseases, "Influenza: Fact Sheet," July 2008. www.nfid.org.

The National Foundation for Infectious Diseases is dedicated to educating the public and health-care professionals about the causes, treatment, and prevention of infectious diseases.

Facts and Illustrations

Can Influenza Outbreaks Be Prevented?

- The World Health Organization states that the most effective way to prevent influenza outbreaks is **vaccination**.

- The influenza vaccine can prevent **70 to 90 percent** of influenza-specific illnesses in healthy adults.

- Among the elderly, the influenza vaccine has been shown to reduce severe illness and complications by up to **60 percent** and prevent up to **80 percent** of influenza-related deaths.

- Influenza vaccines can protect against infection from type A and B influenza viruses, but not against **type C** viruses.

- The most serious side effect that can occur after influenza vaccination is an **allergic reaction** in people who have a severe **allergy to eggs**, since the viruses used in the vaccine are grown in hens' eggs.

- By executive order of the president of the United States, **federal isolation and quarantine** may be authorized for illnesses that might result in pandemics. These include influenza, cholera, diphtheria, tuberculosis, plague, smallpox, yellow fever, viral hemorrhagic fevers, and severe acute respiratory syndrome.

- Vaccination is the main defense against influenza, but because the viruses mutate easily and rapidly, vaccination **does not guarantee 100 percent immunity**.

H1N1 Vaccine Distribution Around the World

The World Health Organization (WHO) coordinated the distribution of donated H1N1 vaccine to countries that needed assistance in preventing the spread of pandemic influenza. Between January and May 2010, WHO had delivered nearly 21 million doses of vaccine to 39 countries. The donated vaccine, syringes, and other related supplies came from governments, foundations, and manufacturers. As of May 2010, WHO had received pledges of approximately 200 million doses of vaccine and 70 million syringes in addition to a U.S. government pledge of $48 million for operations.

Completed Vaccine Deliveries (1 January–3 May, 2010)

Country	# of Doses	Arrival	Country	# of Doses	Arrival
Afghanistan	500,000	22 Feb.	Mongolia	270,000	29 Mar.
Lao	600,600	25 Feb.	Guyana	75,000	29 Mar.
PN Guinea	700,000	26 Feb.	Guatemala	260,000	30 Mar.
Togo	132,000	27 Feb.	Philippines	1,900,000	30 Mar.
Nauru	1,000	27 Feb.	Tuvalu	1,000	30 Mar.
Maldives	31,200	2 Mar.	Azerbaijan	344,000	1 Apr.
Fiji	88,200	3 Mar.	Bolivia	900,000	2 Apr.
Nicaragua	110,000	3 Mar.	Myanmar	972,000	4 Apr.
Tonga	10,000	3 Mar.	Suriname	50,000	15 Apr.
Vanuatu	25,000	3 Mar.	Seychelles	9,000	21 Apr.
Kiribati	10,000	4 Mar.	Timor-Leste	117,000	21 Apr.
Solomon Is.	55,000	4 Mar.	Liberia	78,000	23 Apr.
Kosovo	100,000	9 Mar.	Niue	1,700	23 Apr.
Cuba	1,124,000	17 Mar.	Bangladesh	3,000,000	27 Apr.
Honduras	140,000	18 Mar.	Sudan	700,000	29 Apr.
Kenya	730,000	24 Mar.	El Salvador	2,276,000	30 Apr.
Cook Is.	2,000	24 Mar.	Georgia	100,000	1 May
Samoa	18,000	24 Mar.	Paraguay	600,000	2 May
Tokelau	200	24 Mar.	Cambodia	1,800,000	3 May
Pakistan	3,100,000	29 Mar.			

Total	39 Countries / 20,930,900 doses

Source: World Health Organization, "Pandemic (H1N1) 2009 Vaccine Deployment Update-3 May 2010," May 2010. www.who.int.

H1N1 Vaccine Distribution in the United States

Vaccination is considered the best way to protect against H1N1 influenza infection. To facilitate vaccine distribution in the United States, federal public health officials allocated vaccine to each state in proportion to its population. State public health officials could then order whatever amounts of vaccine they felt were needed for their states. Between December 2009 and January 2010 millions of doses of vaccine were allocated, ordered, and shipped in the United States.

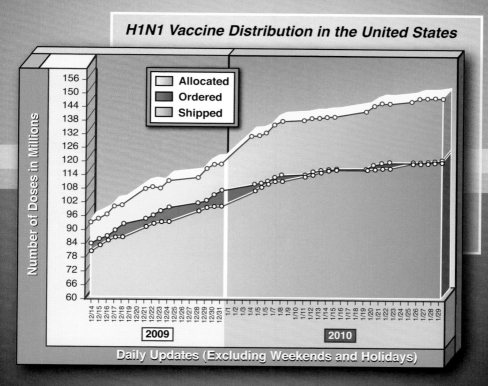

H1N1 Vaccine Distribution in the United States

Source: Flu.gov, "2009 H1N1 Vaccine Doses Allocated, Ordered and Shipped by Project Area Archives Posted October 16, 2009–January 28, 2010," 2010. www.flu.gov.

- Children under nine often need **two doses** of seasonal influenza vaccine, given approximately one month apart, rather than the usual single dose.

Seasonal Flu Vaccines Most Common Among Elderly

According to the Centers for Disease Control and Prevention, people 65 years and older are more likely to get seasonal flu vaccines than any other age group and the percentage of elderly who get these vaccines has been fairly steady. For several years, public health officials recommended seasonal flu vaccines primarily for people in that age group but that recommendation was expanded in 2001 to include people 50 years of age and older. Public health officials usually recommend vaccination for younger adults only if they are health care workers, if they are in close contact with people who are likely to contract influenza, or if they have high-risk health conditions.

Percentage of adults aged 18 years and over who received an influenza vaccination during the past 12 months, by age group and quarter: United States, 1997–2008

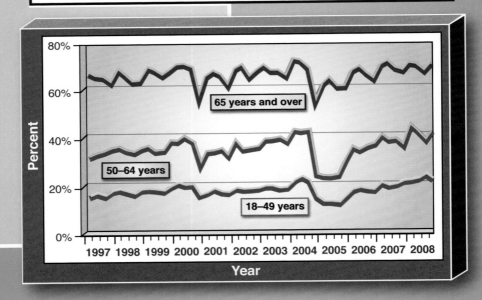

Source: Centers for Disease Control and Prevention, "Early Release of Selected Estimates Based on Data from the 2008 National Health Interview Survey," June 24, 2009. www.cdc.gov.

- The National Foundation for Infectious Diseases states that because **influenza viruses change from year to year** and new variants arise, annual flu vaccination is necessary to prevent infection.

- Each September the World Health Organization analyzes influenza strains circulating in the **Southern Hemisphere** before selecting the ones to include in the next flu season's vaccine, and it does the same for the **Northern Hemisphere** each February.

- The H1N1 vaccine does not protect against seasonal strains of influenza.

- According to the U.S. Department of Health and Human Services, very little is known about the benefits of wearing **face masks** to help control the spread of influenza in community settings.

Key People and Advocacy Groups

American Lung Association: An agency that seeks to improve lung health and prevent lung disease through education, advocacy, and research.

Christopher Andrewes, Wilson Smith, and Patrick Laidlaw: British physicians who proved that human influenza was caused by viruses and not bacteria, as was previously believed.

Centers for Disease Control and Prevention: An agency of the U.S. Department of Health and Human Services that is charged with promoting health and quality of life by controlling disease, injury, and disability.

Childhood Influenza Immunization Coalition: An organization whose mission is to protect children's health by improving low influenza immunization rates.

Families Fighting Flu: A group that works toward improving the rates of childhood flu vaccinations and helping reduce the number of childhood illnesses and deaths caused by influenza.

Thomas Francis: An American microbiologist who was the first to conclude that more than one strain of influenza virus exists. He isolated virus types A and B and was also the developer of the first influenza vaccine.

Immunization Action Coalition: An organization that seeks to increase immunization rates and prevent disease through education and awareness.

National Institutes of Health: The leading medical research agency in the United States.

Richard E. Shope: An American physician who isolated the influenza virus from infected pigs and confirmed that swine influenza was caused by a virus rather than bacteria; his work was the stepping-stone for later discoveries about human influenza.

Jeffery K. Taubenberger: A virologist with the National Institutes of Health who is a world-renowned influenza expert.

R.M. Taylor: An American physician who isolated influenza type C.

U.S. Department of Health and Human Services: The cabinet department of the U.S. government responsible for protecting the health of all Americans.

World Health Organization: The directing and coordinating authority for health within the United Nations system.

Chronology

1580
The first documented global influenza outbreak originates in Russia, then sweeps through Europe, killing thousands of people in Italy and nearly wiping out the entire population of several Spanish cities.

1940
American microbiologist Thomas Francis identifies influenza virus type B.

1918
A devastating strain of influenza, which comes to be known as Spanish flu, sweeps through Europe, Asia, Africa, North America, and the South Pacific, killing 20 million to 100 million people worldwide.

1890
Russian flu, which began in central Asia in 1889, results in 500,000 to 750,000 deaths worldwide.

1500   **1900**   **1920**   **1940**

1892
German bacteriologist Richard Friedrich Johannes Pfeiffer identifies a bacterium that he isolated from flu-infected patients and erroneously concludes that influenza is caused by bacteria.

1930
American physician Richard E. Shope isolates the influenza virus from infected pigs and confirms that swine flu is caused by a virus; he suspects the same may be true of influenza that affects humans.

1933
British physicians Christopher Andrewes, Wilson Smith, and Patrick Laidlaw isolate the flu virus from infected humans, thus confirming Richard E. Shope's theory that influenza is caused by viruses and not bacteria.

1934
American microbiologist Thomas Francis becomes the first to conclude that more than one strain of influenza virus exists, and he identifies virus type A.

Chronology

1941
The U.S. Navy conducts a mass experiment with sailors and demonstrates that influenza can be controlled by a vaccine.

2010
The Centers for Disease Control and Prevention estimates that 2009 H1N1 influenza has killed from 8,870 to 18,300 people in the United States since April 2009.

1957
As much as 35 percent of the world's population is infected by an influenza pandemic that begins in China and spreads to Europe and the United States, eventually killing about 2 million people.

2009
After an outbreak of H1N1 influenza occurs in Mexico and begins to spread rapidly, the World Health Organization issues the first pandemic alert of the twenty-first century.

1940

1975

2010

1949
American physician R.M. Taylor identifies influenza virus type C.

1997
An H5N1 influenza virus that originated in poultry spreads through Hong Kong and kills six people, marking the first time a flu virus has been transmitted directly from birds to humans.

1968
An outbreak of influenza known as the Hong Kong flu originates in southern China and sweeps around the world, claiming an estimated 1 million lives.

2005
After analyzing preserved tissue from several people who died in the 1918 Spanish flu pandemic, scientists are able to reconstruct the influenza virus strain that caused the disease.

Related Organizations

American Lung Association

301 Pennsylvania Ave. NW

Washington, DC 20004

phone: (202) 785-3355 • fax: (202) 452-1805

e-mail: info@lungusa.org • Web site: www.lungusa.org

The American Lung Association seeks to improve lung health and prevent lung disease through education, advocacy, and research. Its Web site features a number of influenza fact sheets, news articles, and reports.

Centers for Disease Control and Prevention

1600 Clifton Rd.

Atlanta, GA 30333

phone: (800) 232-4636

e-mail: cdcinfo@cdc.gov • Web site: www.cdc.gov

An agency of the U.S. Department of Health and Human Services, the Centers for Disease Control and Prevention seeks to promote health and quality of life by controlling disease, injury, and disability. Its Web site offers a wealth of information about seasonal influenza, including an extensive Flu Topics section, fact sheets, a map of influenza activity in the United States, an *Influenza: The Disease* publication, videos and podcasts, and links to other flu-related Web sites.

Childhood Influenza Immunization Coalition

139 Fifth Ave., Floor 3

New York, NY 10010

phone: (212) 886-2277

e-mail: ciic@nfid.org • Web site: www.preventchildhoodinfluenza.org

The Childhood Influenza Immunization Coalition seeks to protect children's health by improving low influenza immunization rates. Its Web site features a variety of fact sheets, an educational influenza video, "Flu

Funnies" videos, Q&A with the Experts, personal stories, and information about the flu vaccine.

Families Fighting Flu

4201 Wilson Blvd., #110-702

Arlington, VA 22203

phone: (888) 236-3358 • fax: (202) 835-8879

e-mail: contact@familiesfightingflu.org

Web site: www.familiesfightingflu.org

Through education and advocacy, Families Fighting Flu seeks to improve the rates of childhood flu vaccinations and help reduce the number of childhood illnesses and deaths caused by influenza. Its Web site features an informational flyer about influenza's effects on children, a Fact vs. Fiction page, news releases, and facts about influenza prevention.

Immunization Action Coalition

1573 Selby Ave., Suite 234

St. Paul, MN 55104

phone: (651) 647-9009 • fax: (651) 647-9131

e-mail: admin@immunize.org • Web site: www.immunize.org

The Immunization Action Coalition seeks to increase immunization rates and prevent disease through education and awareness. Its Web site offers news releases and articles, photographs, influenza videos, questions and answers about influenza, case histories of people who have died from influenza, and additional references.

Infectious Disease Society of America

1300 Wilson Blvd., Suite 300

Arlington, VA 22209

phone: (703) 299-0200 • fax: (703) 299-0204

e-mail: info@idsociety.org • Web site: www.idsociety.org

The Infectious Disease Society of America represents physicians, scientists, and other health-care professionals who specialize in infectious diseases. Its Web site offers influenza fact sheets, news releases and articles, and the *IDSA News* publication.

National Foundation for Infectious Diseases

4733 Bethesda Ave., Suite 750

Bethesda, MD 20814

phone: (301) 656-0003 • fax: (301) 907-0878

e-mail: info@nfid.org • Web site: www.nfid.org

The National Foundation for Infectious Diseases is dedicated to educating the public and health-care professionals about the causes, treatment, and prevention of infectious diseases. Its Web site features a variety of publications and fact sheets about influenza and vaccines, Key Facts & Figures, and influenza public service announcements.

National Institutes of Health

9000 Rockville Pike

Bethesda, MD 20892

phone: (301) 496-4000

e-mail: NIHinfo@od.nih.gov • Web site: www.nih.gov

The National Institutes of Health is the leading medical research agency in the United States. Its Web site search engine produces nearly 8,000 articles about influenza, as well as links to the separate National Institute of Allergy and Infectious Diseases site, which offers an extensive array of influenza-related information.

Public Health Agency of Canada

1015 Arlington St.

Winnipeg, Manitoba R3E 3R2

phone: (204) 789-2000 • fax: (204) 789-7878

Web site: www.phac-aspc.gc.ca

The Public Health Agency of Canada is the government's principal agency to promote public health in Canada. Its FluWatch Web site offers weekly influenza reports, news releases, facts about vaccinations, and an extensive list of alphabetized publications.

U.S. Department of Health and Human Services (HHS)

200 Independence Ave. SW

Washington, DC 20201

phone: (877) 696-6775

Web site: www.flu.gov

The U.S. Department of Health and Human Services is the government's principal agency for protecting American's health and is the managing sponsor of Flu.gov. The Web site offers extensive information about influenza including various types, prevention and treatment, an interactive timeline of the 2009 H1N1 influenza pandemic, a link to a blog, and a searchable database for frequently asked questions.

U.S. Food and Drug Administration (FDA)

10903 New Hampshire Ave.

Silver Spring, MD 20993

phone: (888) 463-6332

Web site: www.fda.gov

The U.S. Food and Drug Administration is charged with protecting public health by ensuring the safety and effectiveness of drugs, vaccines, medical devices, food, and other products. Its Web site's searchable database produces nearly 4,300 influenza-related publications.

World Health Organization (WHO)

Avenue Appia 20

1211 Geneva 27

Switzerland

phone: 41 22 791 21 11 • fax: 41 22 791 31 11

e-mail: info@who.int • Web site: www.who.int/en

The World Health Organization is the directing and coordinating authority for health within the United Nations system. The Health Topics section of its Web site produces fact sheets, information on disease outbreaks and pandemics, recommendations for influenza vaccines, and data/statistics.

For Further Research

Books

Roni K. Devlin, *Influenza*. Westport, CT: Greenwood, 2008.

Patricia J. Fanning, *Influenza and Inequality: One Town's Tragic Response to the Great Epidemic of 1918*. Amherst: University of Massachusetts Press, 2010.

Connie Goldsmith, *Influenza*. Minneapolis, MN: Twenty-first Century Books, 2010.

Dorothy Ann Pettit, *A Cruel Wind: Pandemic Flu in America, 1918–1920*. Murfreesboro, TN: Timberlane, 2008.

Tom Quinn, *Flu: A Social History of Influenza*. London: New Holland, 2008.

Delthia Ricks, *100 Questions & Answers About Influenza*. Sudbury, MA: Jones and Bartlett, 2009.

Terence Stephenson, *Swine Flu/H1N1: The Facts*. London: Jessica Kingsley, 2009.

Periodicals

Amanda Gardner, "A Year After Its Emergence, H1N1 Swine Flu Lingers," *Business Week*, June 4, 2010.

Donald F. Groce, "Stop Pandemic Progress . . . Start with Your Hands," *Industrial Safety & Hygiene News*, February 2010.

Betsy McKay, "The Flu Season That Fizzled," *Wall Street Journal*, March 2, 2010.

Jim Motavalli, "Lessons from Swine Flu: The Once-Looming Public Health Threat Has Receded . . . but We're Still Understanding Our Role in Such Outbreaks," *E*, May/June 2010.

Anahad O'Connor, "The Claim: Flu Viruses Live Longer on Surfaces than Cold Viruses," *New York Times*, December 14, 2009.

Arthur Reingold, "Hand-Washing Won't Stop H1N1," *Newsweek*, September 15, 2009.

Avi Salzman, "What If a Flu Like 1918's Broke Out Now?" *New York Times*, March 23, 2008.

Michael Scherer and Eben Harrell, "Inside the Fight Against a Flu Pandemic," *Time*, August 12, 2009.

Steve Sternberg, "One Year Later: Pandemic Is Over, but H1N1 Flu Remains Active," *USA Today*, April 21, 2010.

Bryan Walsh, "One Year Later: 5 Lessons from the H1N1 Pandemic," *Time*, April 27, 2010.

Arlene Weintraub et al., "Lessons from the Pandemic That Wasn't," *BusinessWeek*, February 15, 2010.

Internet Sources

American Lung Association's Influenza Prevention Program, "Faces of Influenza," 2010. www.facesofinfluenza.org.

Centers for Disease Control and Prevention, "Seasonal Influenza: The Disease," June 3, 2010. www.cdc.gov/flu/about/disease/index.htm.

Discovery Health, "Colds & Flu Center," 2010. http://health.discovery.com/centers/coldsflu/coldsflu.html.

Miriam Falco, "H1N1 Virus' Death Toll as High as 17,000, CDC Estimates," CNN, February 12, 2010. www.cnn.com/2010/HEALTH/02/12/h1n1.deaths/index.html.

Meghan Lewit, "How Influenza Evades the Body's Defenses," *USC News*, May 20, 2009. www.usc.edu/uscnews/stories/16555.html.

Medical Teaching Foundation, "Influenza," History of Medicine Series, 2010. www.historyofinfluenza.com.

Madison Park, "On H1N1 Anniversary, a Mother Lives Daily with Regret," CNN, April 26, 2010. www.cnn.com/2010/HEALTH/04/26/h1n1.one.year.anniversary/index.html.

U.S. Department of Health and Human Services, *Pandemic Influenza Storybook: Personal Recollections from Survivors, Families, and Friends.* www.pandemicflu.gov/storybook/credits.html.

World Health Organization, "Avian Influenza," 2010. www.who.int/csr/disease/avian_influenza/en.

Source Notes

Overview

1. Quoted in WBNS-TV News, "Family Remembers Mother Who Died from H1N1 Virus," September 7, 2009. www.10tv.com.
2. National Institute of Allergy and Infectious Diseases, "Flu (Influenza)," October 13, 2008. www.niaid.nih. gov.
3. Centers for Disease Control and Prevention, "Misconceptions About Influenza and Influenza Vaccine," January 22, 2008. www.cdc.gov.
4. Charles Davis, "Flu (Influenza, Conventional and H1N1)," MedicineNet, October 29, 2009. www.medicinenet. com.
5. Delthia Ricks, *100 Questions & Answers About Influenza*. Sudbury, MA: Jones and Bartlett, 2009, p. 13.
6. Terence Stephenson, *Swine Flu/ H1N1: The Facts*. London: Jessica Kingsley, 2009, p. 13.
7. Ricks, *100 Questions & Answers About Influenza*, p. 7.
8. Ricks, *100 Questions & Answers About Influenza*, p. 7.
9. Roni K. Devlin, *Influenza*. Westport, CT: Greenwood, 2008, p. 23.
10. Devlin, *Influenza*, p. 68.
11. Ricks, *100 Questions & Answers About Influenza*, p. 17.
12. James M. Steckelberg, "Flu Germs: How Long Can They Live Outside the Body?" Mayo Clinic, December 19, 2009. www.mayoclinic.com.
13. Anne Schuchat, a participant in "CDC 2009 H1N1 Flu Media Briefing," Centers for Disease Control and Prevention Press Briefing Transcript, March 29, 2010. www.cdc.gov.
14. Devlin, *Influenza*, pp. 79–80.
15. Devlin, *Influenza*, p. 60.
16. Centers for Disease Control and Prevention, "Estimating Deaths from Seasonal Influenza in the United States," September 4, 2009. www.cdc. gov.

What Is Influenza?

17. Ricks, *100 Questions & Answers About Influenza*, p. 4.
18. Gillian K. SteelFisher, Robert J. Blendon, Mark M. Bekheit, and Keri Lubell, "The Public's Response to the 2009 H1N1 Influenza Pandemic," *New England Journal of Medicine*, May 19, 2010. http://content.nejm. org.
19. Stephenson, *Swine Flu/H1N1*, p. 17.
20. Stephenson, *Swine Flu/H1N1*, p. 17.
21. Quoted in Science Daily, "Pandemic Flu Can Infect Cells Deep in the Lungs," September 11, 2009. www. sciencedaily.com.
22. Quoted in Gina Kolata, "Study Shows Why the Flu Likes Winter," *New York Times*, December 5, 2007. www.ny-times.com.
23. Quoted in Kolata, "Study Shows Why the Flu Likes Winter."
24. Quoted in Science Daily, "Does Winter Cause the Flu?" January 1, 2008. www.sciencedaily.com.
25. Quoted in Madison Park, "H1N1: Pandemic Was Emotional as Well as Physical," CNN, February 23, 2010. www.cnn.com.
26. Luke Duvall, "Beating the Odds," Shot of Prevention blog, December 9, 2009. http://shotofprevention.com.
27. Duvall, "Beating the Odds."
28. Duvall, "Beating the Odds."
29. Duvall, "Beating the Odds."

30. Duvall, "Beating the Odds."

What Causes Influenza?

31. Jeffery K. Taubenberger, Johan V. Hultin, and David M. Morens, "Discovery and Characterization of the 1918 Pandemic Influenza Virus in Historical Context," *Antiviral Therapy*, 2007. www.ncbi.nlm.nih.gov.
32. Devlin, *Influenza*, pp. 5–6.
33. Devlin, *Influenza*, p. 12.
34. Ricks, *100 Questions & Answers About Influenza*, p. 101.
35. Devlin, *Influenza*, p. 26.
36. Ricks, *100 Questions & Answers About Influenza*, p. 100.
37. David Brown, "Swine Flu Wanes, but Experts Say Pandemic Strain Could Reemerge," *Washington Post*, February 23, 2010. www.washingtonpost.com.
38. Quoted in Don Sapatkin, "'Very Eerie': This Winter Had Virtually No Flu," *Philadelphia Inquirer*, April 13, 2010. www.philly.com.
39. Quoted in Thomas H. Maugh II, "Swine Flu Outcompetes Seasonal Flu, Unlikely to Get More Lethal," *Los Angeles Times*, September 1, 2009. http://latimesblogs.latimes.com.
40. Quoted in Amanda Gardner, "A Year After Its Emergence, H1N1 Swine Flu Lingers," HealthFinder, June 4, 2010. www.healthfinder.gov.

What Are the Public Health Risks of Influenza?

41. Quoted in Elizabeth Landau, "1918 Flu Survivors Share Memories as Research Continues," CNN, May 4, 2009. www.cnn.com.
42. Devlin, *Influenza*, p. 32.
43. Devlin, *Influenza*, p. xxii.
44. President's Council of Advisors on Science and Technology, *Report to the President on U.S. Preparations for 2009-H1N1 Influenza*, August 7, 2009. www.whitehouse.gov.
45. President's Council of Advisors on Science and Technology, *Report to the President on U.S. Preparations for 2009-H1N1 Influenza*.
46. SteelFisher et al., "The Public's Response to the 2009 H1N1 Influenza Pandemic."
47. Ricks, *100 Questions & Answers About Influenza*, p. 128.
48. Ricks, *100 Questions & Answers About Influenza*, pp. 26–27.
49. Stephenson, *Swine Flu/H1N1*, p. 34.
50. Quoted in Science Daily, "Virus Hybridization Could Create Pandemic Bird Flu," February 24, 2010. www.sciencedaily.com.
51. Deborah Mackenzie, "Universal Vaccine Could Put an End to All Flu," *New Scientist*, August 21, 2009. www.newscientist.com.
52. Margaret Chan, "World Now at the Start of 2009 Influenza Pandemic," news release, World Health Organization, June 11, 2009. www.who.int.
53. Quoted in Rachel Gleeson, "Deadly Swine Flu Risk to Pregnant Women Uncovered in Landmark Study," University of Sydney News, March 19, 2010. www.usyd.edu.au.
54. Quoted in Suzan Clarke, Raquel Hecker, and Sabrina Parise, "'Miracle' Mom: Swine Flu Almost Killed Pregnant Woman," ABC News, October 15, 2009. http://abcnews.go.com.
55. Devlin, *Influenza*, p. 54.

Can Influenza Outbreaks Be Prevented?

56. Quoted in Paul Gabriel, "How Mexico Licked the Flu," *Sunday Star*, August 16, 2009. http://thestar.com.
57. Quoted in Gabriel, "How Mexico Licked the Flu."
58. Ricks, *100 Questions & Answers About Influenza*, p. 100.

59. SteelFisher et al., "The Public's Response to the 2009 H1N1 Influenza Pandemic."

60. Stephenson, *Swine Flu/H1N1*, p. 130.

61. Steve Sternberg, "Lessons from the Swine Flu Pandemic," *USA Today*, April 21, 2010. www.usatoday.com.

62. Jill Matthews, interview with author, May 15, 2010.

63. Centers for Disease Control and Prevention, "Antiviral Drugs for Seasonal Flu," September 8, 2009. www.cdc. gov.

64. Jennifer Sereno, "FluGen Inks Deal for Technology to Stop Virus in Its Tracks," *Wisconsin Business*, June 8, 2010. www.wisbusiness.com.

65. Devlin, *Influenza*, p. xxii.

List of Illustrations

Index

Note: Boldface page numbers refer to illustrations.

About the Author

Peggy J. Parks holds a bachelor of science degree from Aquinas College in Grand Rapids, Michigan, where she graduated magna cum laude. An author who has written more than 90 nonfiction educational books for children and young adults, Parks lives in Muskegon, Michigan, a town that she says inspires her writing because of its location on the shores of Lake Michigan.